How to Build This
Log Cabin
for $3,000

By John McPherson
(with lotsa help from Geri!)

Graham —

with the Pog trees Available
on Ca You wouldn't need As
many —
Enjoy

Prairie Wolf
John & Geri McPherson
POB 96 · Randolph, KS 66554

How to Build This
Log Cabin
for $3,000

ISBN 0-89745-980-6

First Printing February 1999

How to Build This

Log Cabin

for $3,000

Other works by John & Geri McPherson include:

- PRIMITIVE WILDERNESS LIVING & SURVIVAL SKILLS
- PRIMITIVE WILDERNESS SKILLS, APPLIED & ADVANCED
- TO A HIGH PLACE (a novel by Geri, finished but not yet in print)

For information on these and any toher works that
they may be working on,
write John & Geri at:

Prairie Wolf
POB 96
Randolph, KS 66554

CONTENTS

CONTENTS (Cont.)

Introduction

I am a result of every person and every event that I have known.

I read something similar to this once ... and how true it is!

Any slight change in my past, the taking of a left turn somewheres instead of a right, at any point in my life could have taken me on a completely different journey. I might never have known the joy of being _this_ me. I might've been another.

I think of this because once when I was in a crowd of people (not usual for me), shopping I believe, (in a mall of all places) ... I had this weird thought ... _what if my life as it was, wasn't?_ I mean, what if I was to wake up, maybe from a coma, and discover that I had taken that left turn? What if all that I have experienced and done was really just a dream? What if I was really ... _normal!_

I chuckle when I envision myself explaining this dream, my life (which has always been my dream), to others "out there".

Throughout this book I keep referring to _"me"_ and _"we"_. Wife Geri makes for the we part. This was my project. I did all planning and decision making, 95% of the logging by myself and 95% of the building by myself. Most all of the photos were taken by me and I did the writing (w/Geri's help in editing). My friend Ivan, Geri and a few drop-ins helped with the other 5%. Geri did most all of the bark removal and chinking ... both very time consuming projects ... probably saving me two months of labor.

I would like to emphasize something here. I don't like most people. That's why I decided many years ago to live the life-style that I do. The more that I have had to come into contact with people during the writing, printing, and marketing of the books that we have done over the years, the more that I have come to respect this decision. Our society has turned into such that I feel rather insulted when anyone might refer to me as average. What I have observed of the "average" person in our society is mediocrity. Sad to say, huh? Just look around you. The average sales person. The average public servant. Yeah! I just "fired", if that's the word, a person the other day whom I hired to do some internet computer work for me. "Sure", he says, "easy job. Only a couple of hours work. I'll have it done in a week". I call a week later ... "Oh, sorry about that. I got sidetracked. Busy you know." Another week later. A message to his secretary and no return call from him. I left a message to forget it and to return my material. Next day it was in my mail box. No note. No apology from him to have wasted two weeks of my time. This has not been an unusual occurrence for us. We wonder how anything at all gets done "out there". The point that I'm trying to make with this paragraph is, I guess, don't depend on anyone else. If you want to do something, just do it. Much faster and easier on the blood pressure to accept that from the beginning. But I suppose that most who would build a log cabin are *individuals* ... their purpose in doing this is to get away from it all and they understand full well what I'm saying. This is just one step further to breaking from dependence on others.

Well, anyhow. Here I am. And this I have done ... the cabin, that is. And I'm going to show you just how I was able to.

I built it for selfish purposes ... to teach a friend ... and in the process, fulfilling a lifelong dream. And, of course, I end up with the building.

"Far better it is to dare mighty things ...
than to take rank with those poor spirits who
neither enjoy much nor suffer much,
because they live in the gray twilight
that knows not victory nor defeat."

Theodore Roosevelt said that. For anyone reading this book who ain't quite convinced yet to follow their dream ... maybe this will provide a nudge.

Like most events in my life, this cabin wasn't really thought out. All the twists and turns that I've taken over the years has brought me here. My friend Ivan and I were in the timber one time and I commented that there sure were a lot of straight trees. He wanted one day to move to the wilderness and build a cabin (he was 13, maybe 14 then). "Let's do it" (build a cabin), says I. "OK", says he.

But events kinda got a ahold of Ivan and he was able to help for only the beginning stages ... you know, life's twists & turns. But that's alright ... got *me* going.

I got the nudge *and* convenient trees. Cedars are being eradicated around here by farmers and ranchers ... they feel grass is needed to fatten cows. *Ha!* Logs are available in abundance for anyone. Free. The only obligation from most landowners is that you cut two for every one you take.

And it began. When laying out dimensions for the foundations, only then did I seriously consider size. I guess that I had in mind a cabin such as a trapper or mountain man mighta built ... small in size. 8' x 8' or 8'x10' was what came to mind. Easily heated, easily built. But when it came time to make the decision, well, I guess I got greedy. Logs were in abundance, and way too long to restrict myself to such cramped quarters. So the size crept until I got to what I considered was where I had a decent enough sized building for a variety of purposes yet small enough that handling logs wouldn't be too much of a chore. One log long enough to cover each wall was another consideration. 14' x 16' was where I stopped. One story (at the beginning), to be done in one season. But! For reasons explained later, I went into a second season of logging ... and also the second story ... which in the long run is better because one roof now covers twice the floorspace ... and the roof is where most of the dollars went.

Speaking of dollars.. Some quick addition. Spikes, $116; doors & windows, $315; chimney & ventilator, $430; roof & other new boughten boards, $1,700. Total ... just a bit over $2,500. I've put all figures that I can come up with and I still stay below three grand. These are real figures. They could've been cut considerably if I had bought used lumber. I stress this because there are many who would doubt that this could be done.

Ivan once heard some guys (middle aged) talking one evening at Possie's Place, our local restaurant, pool hall and bar. One fellow, it appears, commented that he wanted to put a small getaway cabin up on a piece of property that he owned. "Can't be done" stresses the other three. "Why you'll have a hundred grand in it before you're done" ... and on they went at lengths to explain the pitfalls to expect if he was to be so foolish. This was a real conversation. Here is where the words *mediocrity* and *individualism* would fit.

Blueprints? I had nothing sketched or drawn out. Books I had read on working with logs twenty years ago and experience gained from whatever building I had done since then (first chapter) was all that guided me. Door here? Fine. Window there? Sure. A second story ? Yeah, why not. And so it went. Timewise, I spent probably right around eight months at this. My body is shot ... worst is my back, which affects everything else. When I spent, let's say, six hours working, either logging or putting them in place, someone with a good back could have accomplished the same in maybe half that time. Someone in good shape could conceivably build a comparable cabin an half the time I did ... *if they stuck with it!*

You don't need to be an engineer, architect,
or a carpenter, to do this.
You just gotta wanta bad enough.

Everything that I feel you need to know to build this is contained here. As with my other writings, I try not to give you *reasons* for doing any certain project. I'm not gonna talk you into doing this. I figure that you already want to or you wouldn't be reading this. I just tell you "how-to". I went over my writing and eliminated everything that I don't think you need to know.

Here's what's left. Go to it.

I Built This ... You Can Too!

I just deleted four pages of text.

I feel that I need to give you, the reader, some background of why and how I did this project. I have the responsibility to get across to you the fact that if I can do this, you can. Four pages was just too much *of me*. Let's see how I can whittle it.

**I've had the desire to not only build a real log cabin
but also to actually live in the woods since I was ten or so.
Mom said it couldn't be done in this day and age.
Well, I done it.**

What's so unimpressive about me that if I can do it, so can you?

Well, to begin with I'm not a big guy. Kinda small really. 5'10", 155 pounds. So size don't make the difference. It's between the ears. Mind-set. Also I'm not really young (in years) any-more, 54. And there ain't much of my body that don't hurt. A back injury is the worse part. When the back don't work, nothing else does either. And from past abuse, just about every one of my joints grinds in pain; knees, elbows, shoulders. To paraphrase an old friend, I ain't as good as I once was but I was once as good as I ever was. Believe me, *If I can do this, you can!*

Unless one directs his or her life towards such an off beat life-style goal early on, it usually don't come about.

The freedom one has when they graduate from high school seldom comes again. No obligations: no bills to speak of and not married with children. Well, in a 'round about way I got a 2nd chance when I was 28. Lotsa soul searching kept leading me back to the wilderness ... and so here I am.

Who are you? One looking for a life in the woods? ... or a person with a coupla acre's in a somewhat secluded

The house pictured here is my first (and fourth) building project, beyond my experience of having spent a summer working free for a friend building a house in return for his knowledge.
The lower walk out basement I began work on in 1977, moving into it in '78 or '79.
That was my first ever building project that amounted to anything.
Geri and I, with the ever present help of our good friend Argel Pultz, erected the milled log upper story during the winter of '90/'91.

The shed (L) that is now used as a barn for our horses and the water tower (R) were my next two experiences with building. The framing lumber for both was cut with a sawmill that I used to have. Note the three courses of logs used at the base of the horse shed ... I had intended to build our main house this way and this was my testing ground. These date to around 1983.

area who wants to put up an inexpensive cabin. Whatever, this book can help you do it.

Special skills needed? Not really. You gotta follow some pretty basic instructions and rules (yep, rules in everything). Knowing something about foundations, level, plumb and maybe square (which you'll learn herein). Working with hand tools will require varying degrees of practice. Experience with a chain saw is a major plus ... this is a tough place to learn ... but it can be done. A coupla days into the project you will probably wonder just why in the hell you are doing such & such a thing. Persevere! Hands will callus and muscles will eventually get used to the unaccustomed workout.

My greatest experience in learning was the summer that I spent working (for free, in exchange

(Above) To round out my building experience, the bedroom addition to our main house came next in about 1993, the deck added on the following year. Putting hedge posts as support for the deck was the same as using pilings for the footings of a main structure. (Right) Lastly, our outhouse was refurbished in 1994.

for the experience and education) for a contractor friend of mine by the name of Harlan Williams. The main things that Harlan stressed were that the entire project literally rests on the foundation. You want that done right; solid, square and level. If you've done your homework right, the rest will pretty much fall into place. As the walls go up, keep everything level, plumb and square (tho square ain't as important in log cabin building). He also taught me that it ain't a *screw up* (not his exact words) if you can fix it. Harlan left us way too soon in 1979. I think of him every time I build something. I like to think that he'd be proud of where he helped me go.

All of the prior experience surely helped me in this latest building. I hope to herein save you much of the groundwork that I went thru. I'm sure that if I attempted this log building with nothing more than what you have at hand, I would have been successful ... tho nothing can replace actual, hands on experience ... especially in the use of a chain saw.

Chapter 2
A Quick Run-Thru

Before we get too far along, lets go thru the entire operation kinda quick like to give you an overview. This book ain't just to show you how _I_ did this particular project but to guide _you_ thru the building of your own ... using this as a guide. Remember thru out ... this book is not a blueprint. I had no blue print in building what's here ... made it up as I went. That's the beauty of working with logs and keeping it simple (not that the two always go together ... you can do some mighty fancy building with logs if you so choose).

Foundation. This is what ties the building into the earth and the cabin literally rests on it. To make further operations easy, this needs to be done right. Square corners (if you're building a rectangular or square cabin), level and solidly placed are the key points. Old time cabins are still in place that are no more than laid up with squarish stone ... many times without even mortar. Pilings can also be used here.

Logging. Suitable timber must be

located and arrangements made to get the logs from there to the building site. Experience with a chain saw is a pretty important prerequisite.

Removing the bark is nothing more than a time consuming affair. It's nice to have help with this.

Laying in of the logs is really simple ... kinda like Lincoln Logs, just more work. Notching in of the corners helps to tie the building together (spikes help even more). The logs must be kept level and plumb as you go up. Setting in beams and joists for a loft or second story isn't really hard ... just another step that requires patience.

The **roof** is treated basically the same as a conventional houses' roof. Getting to that point may be a bit different as you have to insure that logs are all in line (pretty much so, anyhow).

Windows and door openings require a special treatment. The logs will settle in time as they cure ... steps have to be taken to protect the windows and doors as they do. In this cabin we installed eight windows and three doors ... so I had plenty of experience by the time I was done. Not hard, just another step that has to be taken care of. None of this is really hard ... once you are shown just *what* and *how-to*.

Tools ... for the most part,

18

nothing out of the ordinary. Most outdoorsmen already have a supply on hand: chain saw, ax, chains, cables, come-a-long. Some specifically designed for logging will come in handy but can be gotten along without.

Chinking ... for the most part, a mindless task. But very time consuming. As with barking, the builder is many hours ahead if someone else can fill in here (fully intended). Geri has probably six weeks of doing not much more than this ... leaving me free to finish the doors and windows. I just about kept ahead of her.

Moving and raising these heavy logs may seem daunting at first, but after studying and coming to understand how, it becomes an easy task.

Chapter 3

Tools

The list is pretty basic. First of all a quality **chain saw** is in order ... 16 to 18 inch bar lengths are just about right. Insure that the engine is powerful enough to pull its load ... yet you want it light enough to handle comfortably, sometimes (all too often) overhead. I used four saws over the course of the two years of actual logging, a luxury that most of you won't have. It's just that we depend on wood for all of our heating and over the years I've accumulated them from various sources. I hate to recommend one brand over another here ... anymore most are built pretty good. Speak to, not necessarily a chain saw dealer, but maybe someone who repairs them. Get some advice. Most real good, quality saws powerful enough to handle the job can be had new for maybe on the plus side of $300.

Chains and **cables** are a must. **Rope** will work but you may find yourself replacing it a lot. A **snatch block** (pulley of sorts) or other means to divert the direction of pull of cable/rope smoothly.

An **ax** or a **hatchet** will come in handy at times. Old time tools such as an **adze** (for cutting flat surfaces from above) and a **broadax** (for flattening logs sideways) remain with us for a reason ... they have proven themselves. If you can find one or the other, fine ... but you can get along fine without also.

Log tongs are a special type of ice tong. They make dragging and lifting of logs easier.

A **cant hook**, or **Peavy** (basically the same - one has a pointy end) are unsurpassed for turning logs - especially when they don't want to.

A **come-a-long** is a hand operated winch that will do amazing things. I used a winch on the front of our truck for most of the heavy moving and lifting - **it all could have been done with the come-a-long**. A block & tackle will also suffice.

Short to medium length **iron pry bars** will find use.

I illustrate these tools not only because of their importance but because they may not be as well known as some of the everyday tools used.

Tongs (below), whether log or ice, will make the constant moving around of heavy logs lots easier.

(Above) A chain ain't necessarily just a chain. A log chain is built different than a regular towing chain. I found this one at a sale ... you can build your own. Logs roll when you are pulling them, either uphill or across country ... chains and cable will twist. This twisting can ruin cables by kinking them and maybe break a chain if too much tension is achieved. A swivel placed in line somewhere will correct this problem. The steel ring at one end makes it easy to make a noose when latching onto logs, especially slippery ones.

The come-a-long (above) will be a general workhorse helping you in felling trees, snaking logs in the field and around the building site as well as raising on the walls. Even if you have a winch, a come-a-long is indispensable for both small and out of the way jobs.

21

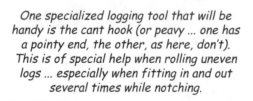

One specialized logging tool that will be
handy is the cant hook (or peavy ... one has
a pointy end, the other, as here, don't).
This is of special help when rolling uneven
logs ... especially when fitting in and out
several times while notching.

A heavy hammer and long spikes. The spikes tie each course of logs together. I used a minimum of four per log. When a log was cut for openings, I used two spikes per section ... so if there was a door and a window, there would be six spikes for that one log section. I countersunk the spikes into the laying log so that five to six inches dug into the log below.

A snatch block (above) ... opens to allow the rope or cable to be inserted ... useful when diverting the direction of pull. Running the cable around a tree makes for tougher pulling and can ruin the rope or cable. A 24' carpenter's level (below) will keep you on line.

Chain Saws

One or more chain saws ain't a must but they sure lighten the load. A purist might scream about not using axes and cross cut saws ... and if so mention using a stone ax. I have. A coupla years back myself and some area teenagers built a 20 foot long dugout canoe using nothing but stone axes and adzes. It can be done ... but my body wouldn't want too much more of it.

Realistically, the modern cabin builder that this manual is written for is going to want to make this as easy a task as possible. A chain saw is the way to go. Two is better, then one can break down or cool off without putting you out of business. A 16 to 18 inch bar (cutting length) is about right. Keep it as light as possible but with enough engine power to handle the job. There are probably 100 logs used in the cabin illustrated. Another 10 or so were cut into boards for the upstairs floor ... an even tougher job on the saws than dropping trees.

The saw will provide you the best service with just some basic care. 1 - Use clean gas, mixed properly with oil. 2 - Don't let the bar oiler run dry. 3 - Keep the air filter cleaned. This minimum service alone should keep the saw(s) up and running for the duration.

Two pretty good saws. The one on the left is pretty heavy duty ... maybe too much so. It weighs a lot more than the other and in the field this hasn't really helped me. For heavier jobs like ripping lumber and bucking heavier firewood it can't be beat. The one on the right I can handle for longer periods of time and it was plenty enough powerful for the logging I put it through. Smaller and lighter pays off when notching logs also. But when the lighter of the two had to go the shop for repairs (a tree fell on it), the other was indispensable.

Keep the chain sharp! A dull chain overworks and overheats both the saw and you. A spare chain kept on hand is a good idea. Keeping the chain sharp is not a big job, especially if done regularly. I touch up the sharpness every two tanks of gas at a minimum. More often whenever. Any chain sharpening guide/file holder will show the proper angle to run the file (insure that you have the proper size file). As you push the file through the tooth, pull into the cutting edge slightly. If the chain is not overly beaten up from hitting rocks & such, just three to five strokes of a **sharp file** will do the job. *Sharp file* is another key phrase ... they're cheap enough at a coupla bucks a throw ... as they quit

Some necessary items for a chain saw first aid kit: one or two extra chains (here one for each of two saws); Screw driver and wrench to free bar and tighten chain; files and file-holder/guides for sharpen-

cutting easily, replace them. Another key rule here ... file each individual tooth the same. Five strokes on one, five strokes on 'em all. If you have one or two badly beaten teeth, they may be taken down further ... but just a coupla. Make especially certain that the angle and number of file strokes are the same from one side to the other. I have to take special care to insure that the same amount of pressure is applied to both sides. I used to apply more from one direction ... pretty soon one side was shorter and the saw would begin to cut in a circle. You want all the teeth to be the same ... or as close as possible.

After each sharpening, the top of the teeth will

lower towards the bar. There is a metal link in front of each tooth called a depth gauge. This keeps the tooth from biting off more than the engine can chew. Literally. At some point you'll note that more pressure is needed to work the saw. Shouldn't be. A properly tuned (sharpened) chain will cut thru wood under its own weight. When it feels like the teeth are not biting as much as possible you need to lower the depth gauges. Simply done by filing with a flat sided file. Not too much, three to four licks to begin with. If too much is removed, you'll have to hold the saw back. Not good. If the first swipes aren't enough, then you can always take a couple more. You can't put the metal back. By the way, the depth gauge checkers that they sell ... well, they never worked for me. I let the saw tell me when its time.

Chapter 4

Barking

Trees have two types of moisture that we need concern ourselves with here. The outside of the tree, the bark, is its raincoat. It keeps the tree's *natural* moisture in. It's the uncontrolled drying out of this natural moisture that makes for logs to crack (check). If the log is protected and the moisture is made to leave at a very slow rate, there will be less, or no, checking. Leaving the bark on and "painting the ends" with some barrier will allow this to happen. Problem here is that this will extend the drying time over a very long time - maybe years.

If the bark is removed, there usually is uncontrolled checking as the moisture leaves. In bow making this can be controlled by using a skill saw (or something such as) and cutting a line along the side of the log that **you want to crack** - this makes the log want to crack at the saw cut.

The bark , if left on, will not only allow for slow drying, but will also allow unnatural moisture (rain, etc.) to get behind it and this will allow the wood to begin to rot. Not desirable. The bark left on also makes for good homes for various wood boring bugs.

So off the bark must come. I cut the trees and put them in place green. The shrinkage and warpage is negligible with eastern red cedar. If using some other, not such ideal wood, other steps might need to be taken. I'll tell you about cedar ... for other woods you'll have to use the library.

Trees live thru cycles, growing differently from year to year depending on climatic conditions. Wet years will see more growth than dry ones. During the late winter and early spring months, the trees begin a new season of growing. Their roots pull water from the earth. At this time thru mid-fall or so, there is enough moisture in the tree so that the bark will peel off easily (I imagine this is so with most species). Sometime during the fall, the sap (natural moisture) begins to leave the tree and its growing season is over ... it becomes dormant. During this period the bark is tightly stuck to the tree.

Photo at left shows squared shovel (spud) slicing and cutting thru bark easily. This was the tool that I pre-ferred when I did any barking as my back don't like bending. The knife shown in photo on the right is what Geri used, and she did most all of this work.

     Geri did most all of the bark removal for this project. I barked a few trees as did a coupla neighboring kids. She did 90%. Each tree was different depending mostly on just how well a job I did of trimming the limbs off in the timber and how many branches there were. On average each log might have required 30 to 40 minutes to skin.

     Late in the season (late Sept. or early Oct.) of our first year of laying logs, I had cut eight logs and drug them here (to the work site). The bark stuck tight. Now the time for debarking one log ran into the hours - anywhere from two to five - per log. Not very efficient.

     By early fall of my first season of log laying I had reached above door level with the walls and had laid in joists for the loft floor. I had hoped to finish the place as a one story workshop the first year of laying. The extra time involved to lay the floor joists level was all the time needed for the bark situation to change. The sap had fallen.

Because of the many extra hours required just to debark, I changed my approach. Too labor intensive for such little gain. I decided instead to use these logs as floor boards for the 2nd floor/ loft. I'll be illustrating this later.

So the logs were barked. Laid up green. Yeah, they'll check as they dry ... and any of the cracks that appear on the outside we'll have to fill with a caulking (or some such thing) to keep from trapping moisture and eventually, all too soon, rotting.

The tool that I found most useful in removing the bark was a small, flat, square ended shovel. The curve tipped "sharpshooter" or "tiling spade" doesn't seem to do the job as well for me. A flatter blade digs in better. A sharpshooter with the end flattened and squared somewhat would be ideal. This type of tool (known among loggers as a spud) is better on the back as you can do the work from a standing position ...

A barking bee. From left; Geri, Dalton Henry (a young neighbor, running partner and sometime helper), and grandsons Travis & Cody.

somewhat. For digging in the low spots and around some of the more stubborn knots, a machete type knife will come in handy.

I normally would begin bark removal by using the edge of the spud to open a crack in the bark along the top of the log ... then feeling, prying, and prodding it's an easy enough job to get the bark to peel off to one, or both, sides. When I got all that I could reach conve- niently, it was a simple matter to roll the log a quarter or half turn and pick up where I left off. If the log curves some and doesn't want to stay in the position you want it to, use a rock or block of wood to hold it in place. It's not really a bad job ... kinda mindless maybe, just needs to get done.

This job and chinking are the times when a helper or two is beneficial .. it takes a lot of time away from the builder for this task. Figure somewhere around 100 logs at 45 minutes per log to debark. That's 75 hours. A bonus to have a helper here.

Chapter 5

Rules

The rules that I followed in building this cabin were really few: 1/ level, 2/ plumb and 3/ square ... and the square part in a log building isn't as important as in conventional structures.

1 - **Level**. You'll want the building to be level to the world. Gravity has the tendency to make things fall and slide *down* and you have to counter this at every step. Level is one counter. When building with logs it would seem that it would be a simple matter of putting large ends against small ends, and after several layers, things will level out. Maybe so ... but ... well, anyhow, lets see.

For the first several layers I did my utmost to insure that each layer was as close to level as I could get it. Why? ... don't know. Just did. I also made it a point to see that there was little or no gap between the logs (something I later judged to be a mistake). Later during the second summer of laying up logs I found that "kinda" level and lotsa gaps were OK. Just keep the "kinda" level within limits ... if one log is a bit off level, make up for it with the next log.

I had a few methods to make my judgements on level. One was simply placing my workaday 24 inch level on the log at various intervals and taking an average (logs around here ain't perfect no matter how good they look ... averaging has to count). A second was to put the level, level, on the opposite wall and look thru the level to the other side. The third was to stand off at a distance and hold the level braced on a coupla sticks (or some such), and again look thru to the log(s). This all might sound kinda simple and crude, but it sure works. Keep level on your mind at each step from the foundation up.

2 - **Plumb**. As important as level, especially when building with logs. No special tools needed ... simply a string with a stone (or other weight) tied at each end. If the foundation is lined out correctly and the first course of

logs anchored to it are on the money, then each log that is laid up needs simply to be centered ... on average! For the first two or three logs going up, the center is more easily found by laying the level at the sides and checking plumb (levels have vertical level bubbles also) ... you'll need a certain height for the string plumb to work, usually three or more logs. Once to this height, use the string plumb regularly and carefully observe. These logs ain't straight, they'll bob & weave. Use the average. It's more important for the logs to be on plumb at window & door openings where you'll later be boxing them in than at the notches where they are self supporting. I've got 20 inch logs sitting on top of six inchers ... and they're solid ... because they are in plumb. The test of how good you did at each step will show when you box in door openings that need to be straight up and down ... mistakes show up well here.

If you stick constantly with these rules thru the laying of each and every log, you'll end at the roof close to the mark.

Chapter 6

Logs

Our cabin was built using only eastern red cedar for logs. At one time I had a book (must've loaned it out) that listed about all woods suitable for log cabin building. It was a chart actually, listing the qualities of many trees used in log cabin building that one would want or need to know before approaching this task. Can't locate it now but what I remember most about this chart was that the rating for eastern red cedar was pretty high. It's light weight (when dried), semi-strong (very flexible), has a good R (insulating) value, a natural insect resistance and most importantly to me, the shrinkage and warpage was right at 1%. In other words, it was pretty much an all around perfect tree for this project. And where we are located in north central Kansas, cedars are considered noxious weeds by most farmers and ranchers.

Neighbor, Russell Peterson, thru whose land our one mile drive runs, has been cutting and burning cedars in cleaning up his pasture for many years. There are a coupla steep ravines out there in which the trees grow straight and tall. Availability of logs was assured. We have also been approached by a few other landowners who had heard of our endeavors, wanting to get rid of trees. Cedar logs in this part of the country are available pretty much for the taking.

Logs straight and long are great if you have them. But as you can see in the accompanying photos of an old timey cabin in the Blue Rapids, Kansas town square, long & straight ain't necessarily needed. My building progress will illustrate some methods of using less than perfect logs but the purpose here is to show you how I done it. If I tried to insert all solutions to all questions that might arise, I'd be researching and writing for a long time to come.

This cabin sits in the town square of Blue Rapids, Kansas.
One look shows much less than perfect logs used in building ... closer observation shows the skilled craftsmanship used in putting it together.

Chapter 7

Logging

Heading to the woods with a chain saw for to cut trees can be dangerous and to make this job safer some basic rules need be understood and followed.

The trail in and out of the ravine where 90% of the second story (& second year's) logs were cut. The hilltop in the distance is where we built and live.

A clean working area is a safer working area. When working in the woods, insure that the immediate area in which you are working is clean - no lumps & other bumpy things to trip over or catch your foot on. A fall with a running chain saw can be deadly! Also insure that any prospective getaway routes are cleared. If the tree decides to go unexpectedly in the wrong direction ... well, make sure you have a gateway thought out. Generally I feel that I'm the safest near the base of the tree that I'm cutting - far enough away so that any sudden kicking back don't get me but close enough to be able to walk around it. The shortest distance to get away from it is there. Keep it clean!

Notching is one of the first skills to master. Trees can be made to fall directionally if approached right. One does not simply take the

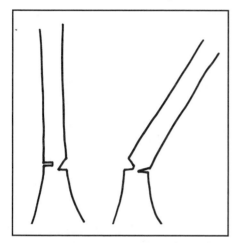

saw and cut straight thru the tree. First a notch is cut on the side of the tree that you want the tree to fall in. Begin by cutting about 1/3rd, or slightly more, of the way thru the tree ... then cut a diagonal line from above to the point where this cut ends (see illustration). This opening, or notch, is to allow the tree to fall freely without binding on itself. To finish the cut, one saws a coupla inches above the notch from the opposite side. If the tree is straight or leaning slightly in the direction of the notch and there is no wind against it, at a certain point the tree will begin to fall. As it does, the material not cut thru between the notch and the back cut will act as a hinge which keeps the tree from kicking up and out as it falls - **another danger!** I watch the notch and "saw kerf" (opening left behind as the saw cuts) carefully. This will tell you what the tree is doing. I cut *slowly* at this point ... if the tree decides to fall backwards, I can sometimes see this happening *at the kerf* and get the saw out before it gets pinched.

If the tree is questionable as to the direction that it will fall, or if your saw does get bound, tie off a rope, chain or cable as high up the tree as you can and run another tie from a tie-off (tree?) in the direction you want/need. Then use a come-a-long or rope & pulley to bend the tree to your will. It can be dangerous to do this hookup after the saw is caught so if in doubt, do it before-hand.

Done before the cutting, take up tension just so that you can visibly see the tree straightening. Make your notch. Then tighten up until the tree is visibly bending in the pulled direction.

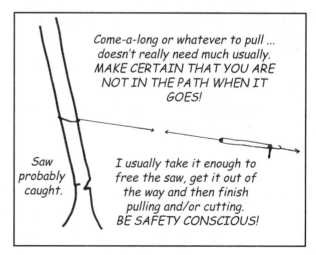

Come-a-long or whatever to pull ... doesn't really need much usually. MAKE CERTAIN THAT YOU ARE NOT IN THE PATH WHEN IT GOES!

Saw probably caught.

I usually take it enough to free the saw, get it out of the way and then finish pulling and/or cutting. BE SAFETY CONSCIOUS!

As you make the cut, watch the kerf carefully to insure that it spreads open.

If done after, to free the saw, work slowly & carefully ... you don't want to pull the tree on top of you. When you see it give just the slightest, get back to the base and remove the saw. Maybe tighten the come-a-long a bit more. Then saw slowly, a bit at a time & watch the kerf. BE SAFE! If the tree falls suddenly in your direction while you're pulling, the safest place might well be at the backside of the tree that you're anchored to - using the tie-off tree to catch the top of the one you're assisting. Be on the lookout for "widowmakers", dead branches from above.

Some of the best trees usable as logs grow densely among others - hence they can be difficult to fell as others are so closely packed as to prohibit this. A hung up tree that has been cut is not only an immediate danger to you but if left as is can likely fall on someone or something else. NEVER LEAVE A TREE IN THIS CONDITION!

Searching out suitable logs is an art. Trees always appear smaller in the woods than when at the building site - the same as with cutting a Christmas tree. It takes a little judgement to for sure know when eight inches is eight inches. I, of course, wanted the logs as long and as straight as possible. Size? Well, as has been pointed out to me, I started with considerably smaller logs than what I ended with. At first I figured that about eight inches at the base with a slight taper would be the ideal ... until I found the nine inchers ... and then the ten inchers ... and more!

When first scouting the areas, I took along an ax or hatchet (& snippers) to open walk areas. Prospective areas I would spend more time cleaning so as to get a better look at the trees. Look up the tree from as low down as you can get. Lay on the ground and look up. Study it carefully. Look for straightness from all sides. Evenness in taper. Sometimes I would cut a forty foot tree and actually take out maybe a ten foot section that fit the bill. The experience of cutting, hauling and putting the logs in place will help your eyes to view trees better. Chances are that the logs that you cut last will be the choicest.

Since good log trees many times are found growing in tight groups, learn how to approach them. If the tree has no place to fall I'll cut it at the base and when it's free I'll attach a line to the base and pull it out - thereby just kinda pulling the bottom of the tree away, having the top end up at or near where the bottom was when it all comes to rest. As the top falls gradually in this situation, I'll trim limbs as they lower themselves to my reach.

When cutting a limb under pressure or when cutting the top off the tree where there is pressure against the wood in one direction, cut thru slightly from the inside of the pressurized limb (if you continue to cut, the pressured wood will bind against the saw) and then finish cutting from the outside. In the case of a tree laying semi flat with the top resting against other trees or brush, the pressured side will be the top - the final cut to be made from the bottom. Always try to stay one step ahead of an accident by trying to predict what the tree or limb will do. Trees and limbs under pressure will act violently sometimes when you free them ... watch to see that your releasing the pressure of a limb on one side doesn't roll the tree on you as a result.

One of the biggest hassles to me when heading to a particular ravine to cut (ravines are where the logs grow best here) is clearing a way in and out. Lotsa brush seems always to be at the treeline and the Eastern Red Cedars that we were using for logs have lots of lower limbs that are springy and space hogs - can hardly crawl thru some of these growths, much less walk. So my first approach was to cut it clean so I could walk to the bottom, which is were I began my cutting. Every time a tree was cut, it left

Cutting off a limb such as this will be commonplace so you need to know how to do it safely. The log is exerting pressure downward ... the limb wants to spring upward. Just be prepared for it to happen all of a sudden. Many times I'll make a slight undercut to help relieve the pressure ... tho it's easy to get the saw caught in a trap if you go too deep. The final cut is made from the top so that the limb is springing away from the chainsaw. I'll make the final trim cut next to the log afterwards. Be prepared for the possibility of the log rolling when pressure of the limb is released.

Top cut

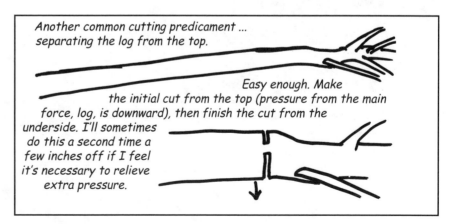

Another common cutting predicament ... separating the log from the top.

Easy enough. Make the initial cut from the top (pressure from the main force, log, is downward), then finish the cut from the underside. I'll sometimes do this a second time a few inches off if I feel it's necessary to relieve extra pressure.

behind lots of leftovers in the form of brush. Something had to be done with it. The landowner here wanted the area cleared of all cedars and was doing most of it thru burning and so piling the leftovers in

A tree line before cleaning an opening.

any particular area wasn't a problem ... but when I cut a tree at the bottom of the hill, I had to eventually snake it to the top ... and thru piles of brush is not the way to do it. So, I would try to read the area

first. But no matter how I tried, piles of brush had to be moved out of the way ... sometimes more than once.

I cut the trees the furthest out (at the bottom of the ravines) first. I could pretty well leave those trimmings as is. Sometimes I would cut three or four before hooking chains onto the logs and dragging them up in tandem. I just had to have a clean area thru which to snake them. The entire hill had to be cleaned so as to walk because I usually had to make this trip a number of times

The same tree line after opening.

Looking downhill from top of the opening.

got me only two or three logs (not all of the trees were suitable for my purposes). Sometimes one clear-cut would provide me with ten or more. Almost the entire second story was taken from the point of a hill at a junction of two ravines. Though it pretty much clear-cut this maybe one acre patch, it took three separate cuts in to get them all out.

My logging was ideal. The land from which I cut adjoined ours. All I had to do was cut them, drag

just to get out one batch of trees; get a come-a-long, an ax or hatchet, chain, cable, canteen, another saw to get me outta trouble when the first one got bound up. I got a workout in more ways than one.

If I did my job right the first time, I would get the first batch or two of logs up with no real problems. But as my cutting advanced up the hillside, I would reach out to the sides and cut trees off of the beaten path - and all too often had to move an earlier brush pile out of the way. Sometimes all of this effort

Looking uphill from the bottom of the ravine. As I cut each individual tree, I'll be constantly moving brush out of my way to so as to have safe movement.

39

Snaking the logs thru the trees isn't really tough ... you just have to guide them in a way that they'll go. Some times I'd have to pull them out one at a time ... other times I could group four or five together. Each trip out was the same, only different.

them up the hill, hook the chain over my ball hitch and drag 'em home. No loading was involved.

In the early '80's I had a small sawmill and was bringing logs in from a coupla miles away. Then I had to cut, drag 'em up the hill, load onto a trailer, bring them here and unload. Lotsa handling. But it can (and is) done. The former situation was better by far.

I would get maybe a dozen or so logs dragged to the building site before it got too crowded and I got to layin'.

Chapter 8
Foundation

As mentioned earlier, a building literally rests on this. The foundation is the buildings contact with the earth. Whether you are building on solid rock or sand, it must be solid. I'll show two types here, the one I used and an alternative. With just this information, you should be able to build in most circumstances. But most importantly, understand the what and why of the foundation ... then you can adjust for your circum- stances.

We live on rock. Limestone and flint (chert) here in the flinthills of Kansas. I put the cabin on top of a hill (for the view, not always a good idea if you're wanting to keep warm). We dug probably no more than 15 to 18 inches before hitting *solid* rock. I mean solid. Two feet or more thick ... and that sits directly on other ledges of rock. So basically, I had it good. But let's start at the beginning.

Site selection. Well, this cabin was built as a workshop and maybe a sort of getaway. Geri rebuilds and works on saddles and collects some tack. We wanted to be somewhat convenient to the house (300 ft. away but out of sight) and also to the horse shed (between the two). I picked a site with a view up the river valley on a spot that would drain water as naturally as

The selected building site ... at the top of a hill with a view up the river valley. We built on the backside of the trees.

We had about the best of all conditions in our selected site as far as foundations are concerned ... a solid rock ledge to build on just under the surface. This exposed face is the remains of an old timey rock quarry. The cabin looks over an island in a reservoir that used to be the town square of old Randolph, Kansas. Many bridges and buildings in the area had rock from here incorporated.

possible, a slightly higher rise. Here, "the draining of water naturally", is the key phrase. Wherever you build, study the site carefully and determine just where all the water would go if suddenly two feet of rain fell. Even in low lands, a slight rise in the ground surface will remain above water. This is the spot to build on. Let the natural runoffs work for you.

That's step one.

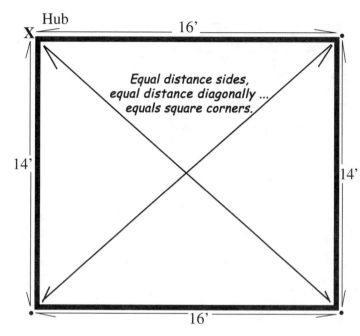

X Hub ── 16' ──

Equal distance sides,
equal distance diagonally ...
equals square corners.

14' — 14'

── 16' ──

(Above) Geri and friend Ivan Anderson stand within the boundary of the marked and dug footings.
(Left) How corners were determined.

Once the actual site was selected, we determined which way to face it. I had already decided on the size (14 x 16 foot). Once I determined the actual position of where the building would stand, I took a long piece of twine and marked off, by tying a knot, at intervals, the size ... 14 ft., 16 ft., 14 ft., and another 16 ft. I had two people helping me but let me describe how one can do this.

Drive a stake in the ground where you know *for sure* one corner will be. This will be your **hub**. Everything else works from the hub. Anchor the beginning of the twine on it (if you tie it, it will be shortened). Looping it on a nail in the stake is OK. Then line the string along where you want the first wall. Plant another stake and let the cord run around the stake or again, a nail at the top. Continue until you arrive back at the hub. Now you have a

14' by 16' rectangle marked off with four stakes (or maybe even just rocks laid as markers). You need to make this rectangle have square corners. Choose whichever wall that you want to be the *hub wall* ... whichever wall faces the direction most important to you. The two stakes at either end of that line are permanent ... hubs. Measure from each of those stakes diagonally to the opposite corner (stake). What you want is for the distance diagonally, corner to corner, to be the same. When the sides (14'x16') are measured and laid out exactly and your diagonal lines are equal, then you are squared.

That's step two.

The footings that I illustrate here, what we actually used, required less than two day's labor for three of us ... not much more for one person. I used the 14x16 foot outline as inside measure-

A closer look up one side of the dug footing. Once sides were trimmed more evenly, the whole was filled with concrete ... with rocks and old hedge posts added as filler. This is the depth we dug to hit solid ledge rock.

ments. Once the marks were double checked, we began digging. The trench was never deep because we hit solid rock soon ... on average probably only 12 to 15 inches deep. We made the trench right at 18 inches wide with square sides ... this is only to be filled with cement so nothing needs be fancy.

The footing will protrude above ground. Now we have another chore facing us ... <u>level</u>. One of the cardinal rules of building. The ground is not necessarily level regardless of how it looks. The building, to literally stand the test of time, needs to be level to the world. So we're gonna make it so.

Determining level can seem like a daunting task ... not so. Place a stake (or use the existing one from outlining the site) solidly at the hub corner. Make a mark on it or use the top, which is more convenient. This mark is your hub from which your roof line is actually determined. This is **the** mark! You now need to place a stake at each of the other three corners on which you will determine a mark which is *exactly the same level as the hub.*

There are many ways in which to determine this, four of which I'll touch on here.

1 - The big boys have an instrument called a transit (a level on a tripod) which is quick and simple to use if you have access to one. Once the tripod is settled (some distance from all marks, the center of the site would work), the level is turned in all directions and adjustments made until the bubble is level whichever way it is turned ... then the level is level to the world. Whichever way the scope (mounted integral with the level) is pointed, anything on the mark in the scope is at the same elevation. Place a marker (stick with a ruler on it) so the bottom of the marker sits on the top of the hub stake. Lets say that when the stick, held straight up and down, when viewed thru the transit shows 56.5 at the mark in the scope. So, where ever the bottom of the stick is, when held straight up and down, and the mark 56.5 (as our example here) is in the window, that's where the exact same level mark is from the hub. Make this mark at all four corners.

2 - Use a water hose. Water finds it own level ... the reason that we build on a slightly higher point than the surrounding land. However long the hose, let all but the two ends lay on the ground. Tie one end to the hub stake so that the end of the hose is at the top of the stake (or wherever your mark is). Fill the hose with water. When you have the other hose end (at another corner stake) adjusted until water is to the top of both ends of the hose, then the two ends are at the exact same level. Repeat this for all corners.

3 - An even more basic way is to put water in the trench until the bottom is covered ... depth isn't a matter but at least an inch or so would insure that you do have *one solid surface of water.* Putting a nail (or stick) in the sides of the trench at the water level will give you an exact level. Simply measure up equal distances from these nails and make a mark on a stake above ground.

4 - What we did. We found 2x4 inch lumber that was straight. Actually we nailed boards together to get this. The important things were that the board was stout enough to span the furthest distance (16 feet) without bowing and that the top was straight. Put one end on the hub stake, adjust the other end until a level placed on the top of the

board showed level. Mark. That's it. We double (and triple) checked this to make sure that all four of the corners were on - even leveling the board diagonally. It might've been primitive, but it worked. All four corners matched.

Now is the time to fill the trench with cement. We used pre-mixed 80# sacks of cement and gravel bought for about $3.00 a bag instead of the smart way of buying a bag of cement at about $6.00 and mixing with gravel or coarse sand. Sand cost us later right at $4.00 a ton ... I can't imagine gravel costing too much more ... just getting it to the site is what I was lazy about. Anyways, fill the trench. In order to make the cement go further we first poured a layer only a coupla inches thick and then added cut lengths of old osage orange fence posts as filler. Old hedge (as osage orange is known as around here) will outlast a person's lifetime when used as posts. I figured that the old posts already had rotted away any parts that would and that using them was the same as using rocks as filler ... which we also did. This ain't just being cheap, it's smart. Square and/or flat rocks laid up have been used in the past for all of this, sometimes not being held in place with cement at all.

Here Geri lays cut sections of old hedge posts in cordwood like fashion. The only mistake that we made here was in not putting enough concrete between for added strength in some spots. Note the string ... level ... used as our guide.

When the trench was filled and we were at ground level, I could have gone up using only cement but that would have involved forming up the sides with wood so as to keep the concrete from flowing away. Mostly because I didn't really feel like going to the extra trouble of doing that, I decided to lay cut pieces of the said hedge posts like cordwood, cementing them in place. The only problem that I can see having resulted from that so far is the fact that I didn't use enough cement around some of the pieces to solidly hold them in place. Most of the "wall" (the above ground portion of the footing, for lack of better wording) is solid enough yet ... it's just that in two of the places where I inserted anchor bolts there wasn't enough cement and one bolt joggled loose while one actually pulled free.

Which brings us to the "anchor bolts". The real thing is an "L" shaped bolt with threads on the long arm. This is set into the footing at various spots to tie the first log into the footing. I used 10 and 12 inch long carriage bolts, or whatever else long enough that I could find, placing large sized washers at the bottom to hold them in. The first log set in place needs to have holes drilled to match the bolts and this is all tightened in place with nuts & washers.

Now if the top of the footing's four sides (walls) are of equal height, there is going to be a space at two ends when you begin laying the first course of logs. You can visualize this by laying two pencils parallel, to simulate logs, on a table top. Then use a pocket knife to notch half way thru two more and lay them as opposing walls. There will be a gap under the last two. What to do? Ha, build two of the walls one half a log (3 to 5 inches) higher. When "cording" the walls, this is a bit simpler than placing an actual half log in, which is an alternative.

Pilings

Another option to tie the building into the earth is the use of pilings. Other than our deck I never have, but I have seen and read about them some. Basically one needs to dig a hole deeper than the frost level ... four to five feet is more than sufficient for anyplace I want to live. This is a good option if you're building in soft soils with nothing solid to tie into and/or you don't want the extra hassle or expense of having to dig and fill deep footings (footings should also be dug below the frost line). Pilings are sometimes the only answer to building on steep slopes. You still need the outline of the building except instead of trenching, you dig post holes at intervals (the spacing ain't cut in stone ... enough to give you solid contact with the earth and close enough together so that the log laid on them will not have the tendency to sag ... certainly one at each corner with some in between). Fill the holes with concrete. You may use some rocks as filler, however I'd think that I'd want the extra strength of solid concrete here. I also think I'd be more comfortable with a larger diameter bottom. The purpose is to end with the piling *tops* level. The *concrete* can quit at any place over six to ten inches or so above ground. If wood is placed on the concrete piling too close to ground level it becomes easier for moisture to affect it (possibly causing rot). If, as in the case of a steep slope, the pilings on one side are a lot taller and you elect not to raise to the level height with concrete all the way, a treated block of lumber (6x6), solid log or even laid up rock can be used to reach level. Whatever, the top of the final pilings, whether wood or concrete, need to be level.

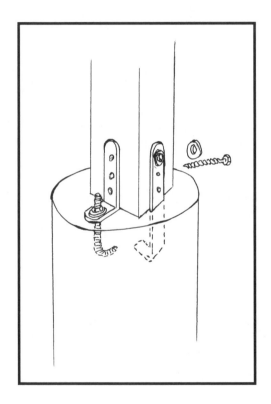

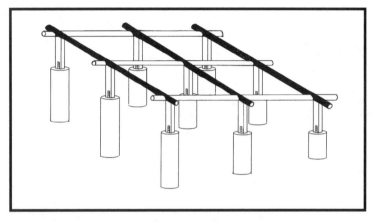

The two drawings on this page will show maybe just a bit better than words what I mean by pilings. Remember, my experience with this is no more than reading about them and having built the deck shown in chapter one. I have seen them. They work! And they may be the most convenient, especially on slopes and out of the way places. Whatever. The illustration at left shows a coupla ways to tie the post (if used) to the piling. These are two different methods tho they can be used together ... it's whatever works! I would use two per ... one each on _opposing_ sides. The drawing above shows how I would lay in the logs. Then take it up at least one more course of logs and lay in floor as shown in the following pages. Don't forget that the logs need to be anchored to the posts in some manner.

Chapter 9
Floor

We left ours dirt. By choice. End of chapter.

• • • • •

But ... if you want to do something different, you can do it now or later. Now especially if you want to pour a concrete floor ... maybe one of the more expensive options (the other being wood, expensive that is). Pouring a concrete floor ain't much for fun, especially inside of a complete building where movements are restricted by walls.

Later is maybe better if you decide to lay flagstone, bricks or use wood. The floor will take a beating in the log building process, at least the way I do it. Lots of heavy stuff falling.

Laying in rock or brick can be as simple as covering the floor several inches (3 to 5) deep with the finest sand that you can get - masonry. Scoop a depression (leaving some at the bottom) and set in a flat stone or brick. Repeat. A lot. You can make patterns with different types and color stone or intermix patterns out of brick with flagstone. No mortar is necessary ... tho if mortar was used it would certainly be more solid ... tho you'll be surprised at just how solid this all sets into the fine sand. Level as you go.

A wooden floor can be had by building a frame of 2x4's (next page) around the perimeter and adding spacers at every 16" (or whatever, it's your floor ... the closer together, the more solid). Level this and nail down floor boards. Tongue & groove is best but more expensive. With the exception of the outer framework, the rest can be all scrap lumber, spaced however ... you'll see where to place nails as you go. I would prefer the dirt floor over this as then I would know that there were no snakes or mice hiding under the floor. With dirt, they gotta be in the cupboards.

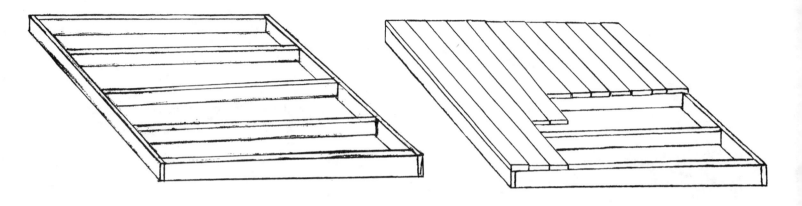

Some quickie sketches of how I'd put a wooden floor into the cabin. The box could sit on the dirt (or in sand) and probably be nailed also to the logs for additional support. Insure level. You could/ might have a termite problem here ... don't know for sure what I'd do ... maybe spread a layer of tin between earth and floor?

For building on pilings the construction would be the same except that I would enclose the bottom (right, lower). Nailing overhead is a bear. I'd use plywood (or some-such) and cut into more manageable strips to fit nailers. Caulking between the strips would keep insects out as well as would thin batting strips nailed over the seams.

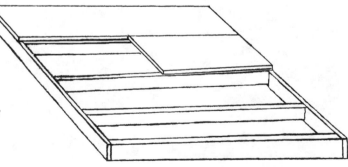

(For clarity, this is illustrated upside down).

51

Chapter 10

Laying Logs

The foundation sat for close to a year before we began to put logs in place. It could have been only several days. The concrete would have cured enough to take the stresses of building in short order. I just didn't get around to it.

The first layer (course) of logs took a bit of measuring and fitting ... remember, the foundation has been built higher at two ends (lower at the other two?!). The first logs go on the low sides. In my case I wanted to have a door on each of the two long (16 foot) sides and I left gaps for these as I went ... I needn't have. It would have gone much

Placing the first course of logs. On the walls with one log running the full distance, front & rear, there are three anchor bolts. On the walls with doors (left & right) there are two anchor bolts for each section of log ... four per wall. We want the logs to be securely tied to the foundation which, in turn, is tied with the earth.

*This photo shows how at some corners there is
no "one log higher than another".
Notching will be covered in depth later.
Note the right wall half again as high as the left.*

faster for me if I had, in fact, laid one log the entire distance and cut the door out later. By leaving an opening, I actually laid two logs ... more time consuming.

First the log was laid alongside of where I wanted it and marks placed where the anchor bolts were. Holes were drilled (brace & bit) for these. Measure carefully and make the holes somewhat oversized ... I believe that these were 3/4 inch diameter. The low side was put in place first ... the anchor bolts not nutted in yet. I then followed by marking and laying in of the end (higher) logs. These had to be notched to fit the first two (lower) logs. When all was just right, we took it all apart. Why? ... for to put a layer of cement under this first course to more permanently tie it in with the foundation. It sticks together somewhat ... tho maybe not as good as glue. But by doing this now I end with a tighter seal than If I wait and do it afterwards. Only now do I tighten *just snu*g the nuts to the anchor bolts.

It's begun!

This is when you'll feel that you're actually doing a log cabin. Lots of home work behind you. But, if it's been done right, the pieces begin to fall in place. From now, there is a lot of repetition. Cut logs. Lay logs. Progress will alternate between seeming to go fast and then slow. Milestones will be reached; getting to the bottom of windows

... and then above. Then you'll be laying logs above the door height. If a second floor or loft is to be included there will be extra time spent placing in joists. Logs will seem to run together. Looking back, much of the laying is a blur ... but studying the walls in the finished cabin, individual logs each have their own memories. Having smashed a finger on one ... pulling the spikes on another because plumb wasn't satisfactory. A few I purposefully put in place when I might not have ... one with a special *bow out* ... one cut three times to make for straight .... these to illustrate how to use much less than perfect logs. Laying a log at ground level isn't much different than laying one eight feet up ... or fourteen feet up.

I'll approach the various steps one at a time. I'll begin with the subjects that you'll need at every step, such as notching, moving and lifting of logs. I'll add others later as you may or may not need them. Some of the logs that I adapted, you may never ...but then again maybe all that you have to work with are "junk logs" ... every adaptation I show might be needed ... and more. Then again, several of the processes I'll illustrate you might not need or use at all. Your situation might call for its own set of rules. Remember, what I know about log cabins came from reading books on the subject some 20 years ago and putting two up. I made a lot of wrong turns that I wouldn't repeat and I'll point them out ... but you may decide that's the way for *you* to go.

Study the basic rules of site selection, foundation, level and plumb. Familiarize yourself with the tools.

Now, lets get to it.

A mis-measurement or bad cut don't always make for waste. Here I had read the level entirely wrong (no drinking involved) and notched where I shouldn't have. Getting back to level required the insertion of the block as a shim. Once spiked thru and all set, nothing was weakened and a log maybe saved.

Keep your working area clean!

This is a must. I was working along one day and happened to look around. It was a mess ... an accident just waiting to happen. I took a picture, cleaned up and moved along.

It was somewhere around this time that I actually took what could have been a pretty serious spill in this same area. While lifting and moving the end of a log (weight maybe around 80#), top heavy as this made me, I lost balance for no apparent reason. As my upper body went forward pushed along by the extra weight, I stepped out with one foot to catch myself (I was walking across the floor boards shown towards the camera) ... and my foot went thru the gap between the log beyond the floor and the first scaffolding board. My other knee hit the board and prevented what could have been a broken, not skinned, shin.

Just thought that I'd point that out.

Notching

Alog cabin is tied together. Each log is locked to the one above and below. Together with the tie in to the earth thru the foundation, you got one tight bundle. Throughout the building, I hammered in ten and twelve inch spikes ... at a minimum of four to a log. The corners further interlock the whole by fitting them together thru notching.

There are several types of notches ... the most complicated, the dovetail, is seen earlier in the photo of the old cabin built in the 1870's in Blue Rapids, Kansas. I work better at function than I do art. Dovetail notching is certainly one of the more secure notches to use but also the most time consuming. The spikes I set at each corner makes up for any loss of strength here.

I used two types of notches. The better of the two is called a saddle notch ... where the bottom of the top log is cut out to fit over the top of the bottom. The other, which name escapes me, is cutting the top of the bottom log to accept the top log. I used the saddle notch whenever it was possible, the other when I had to. Sometimes both were used in conjunction, kinda like "Lincoln Logs". The saddle notch is preferred simply because it sheds water the best. Whenever a cut is made into the lower log you are inviting moisture to enter and if means aren't taken to counter this (more work), then rot is likely to set in.

My notches were either flat or round bottomed depending on the log below ... round of course for round logs and flat (which was easier) for flatter logs or when both were notched. Both were started the same. I first sighted along the length of the log to be notched (which was turned bottom up) and made a mark with the saw at each side. Cuts were made at the marks (sides) to kinda match the log below ... rounded or square. Saw cuts at intervals between made removal of the wood not difficult with use of an ax, hatchet or adze.

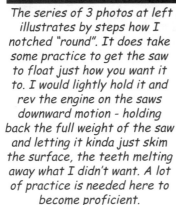

The series of 3 photos at left illustrates by steps how I notched "round". It does take some practice to get the saw to float just how you want it to. I would lightly hold it and rev the engine on the saws downward motion - holding back the full weight of the saw and letting it kinda just skim the surface, the teeth melting away what I didn't want. A lot of practice is needed here to become proficient.

The series on the right show the same for the square cut notch. This is easier to make tho not nearly as good a water shedder because of notching into the log below ... and tho I made faster time with this type notch, I preferred not to use it as much. Practicing these techniques on scrap logs before actual notching would be wise.

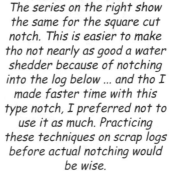

The three photos at left illustrate how to handle the log ends beyond the notch when they stick up high enough to interfere with the laying of the next log. I first scored at intervals with the saw and then removed wood until there was room for the next log to follow. The score lines were cut at an upward bevel so as to shed moisture (this will be covered further in depth in a later chapter dealing with this problem) ... but some attention needs to be paid
at this stage just to continue.

The photo of me below I include here just to show that I actually did some work. The problem with being the photographer is that I'm never in the shots and one might begin to doubt that I'm even here.

Straight, Level & Plumb

Having the final roof line come out level, or at least close to it, you will need to constantly monitor your progress with each log. Steady the level by some means (tied to a log is shown here above) and look through it to the log(s) in the distance. Here I was checking the level of the top of the two gables prior to placing in the main purlin (roof support) by running a rope across between them and checking its level. In the photo at left I was determining the straightness of logs in relation to the top of the log below (which was level) by laying out a section of tape measure ... anything straight (pencil, nail, etc.) can be used. Straightness, level and plumb have to be gauged over the entire length of each individual log and an average taken. Bracing the level on the top of a stick or board will work if done carefully. Two tied or held together is better support. Sometimes I could brace one end against a tree trunk, float the other until the bubble was on, then look thru to the log(s).

(Right) Plumb works with level to make the final building right on. Every log has to be plumbed as well as leveled at each stage. Something as simple as a string with a rock tied at each end will keep the logs going up straight. Remember tho, many logs are not straight and so the plumb, like level, needs to be taken at intervals along the wall to find the right compromise. Being straight up and down at doors and windows will prove to be beneficial later on when framing these in, while some fudging can be done at the corners where the walls are more strong from being tied in with a cross wall.

Fitting Logs Tightly

Sometimes you might want a tight fit between logs ... I know that I did when I began, changing my tactics only when I felt that I would prefer more room for mortar to adhere so as to help hold itself in place. When there is little or nor daylight between the logs you have to put nails or something similar for the mortar to grab onto. So what I have is a combination of many tactics.

The photos below show one log ready to lay that has several points of contact along the way. With the saw (top photo at right) I cut the points of contact out leaving (lower right) a more matching set of logs faces. The logs are shimmed apart during this operation so that the saw doesn't get compressed and is left so in the bottom right photo to more better illustrate the even spacing.

Log with a Hook

I put this log in (L) just because it had character. I could have more easily cut it in front of the crook and spliced in a second log. This was a bit more trouble to chink around (just ask Geri) but leaves us with a bit of a shelf on the inside (R). When chinking, Geri found a scrap piece, had me trim it to length and cemented that in place with enough slope to drain rain (Middle).

What I done here was to lay in a curled log. It was easier for me to lay this as one piece and then cut it than it was to cut it first and lay it twice. See if you can follow this line of thought.

Bent Logs

The log is placed just to the side of where it is gonna finally rest (L), upside down for to be notched ... the other end already is. Note that the other end is parallel to the wall for the notch to be cut. Then the log is shifted (R) so that this end is parallel to the wall for this notch to be cut ... all this time the log is one piece and touches at both ends making it much easier for me to move around.

(Top) The log is then secured into position with a chain to catch the ends in case they fall, a block set to absorb the weight of the two ends that I then create by cutting in two at the area of the bend. I then set the two notches in place, double check plumb and level, set two spikes for each end (trying to miss where I guess window may fit) and this section is done (R).

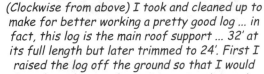

Hewing

(Clockwise from above) I took and cleaned up to make for better working a pretty good log ... in fact, this log is the main roof support ... 32' at its full length but later trimmed to 24'. First I raised the log off the ground so that I would have less chance of my saw cutting dirt and rock, and didn't have to bend my back as much, by jossling with the cant hook and pry bar. I then study carefully to insure that it is indeed straight ... this is easier to see if a straight edge of some type is used, here my tape measure. I then ran a string along each edge to guide my cutting and scoring ... some of the bumps & knots I just sawed off, other sections, where more wood was to be removed, I scored with the saw and removed the remaining sections with the broad hatchet (from the sides) or the adze (from the top). The resulting log when in place looks and performs wonderfully ... very little additional work was required to fit the roof/ceiling boards.

Splicing

Splicing two logs together gives you the advantage of building longer walls than you otherwise might be able to. It also allows you to use two (or more) "good", straight logs where you might hafta do with one "not so good".

If using cured logs, as we did when we built our main house, logs can simply be butted together with caulking gooped between. Also note the "V" Splice used in the 1870's cabin shown on the final pages of this book. Here, where I was using green logs and I wanted the insurance that they would stay together as one as they dried. I did this by cutting ledges that mated at the two ends meeting, securing with a coupla lag bolts and then spiking on either side. Any gaps were filled with caulking.

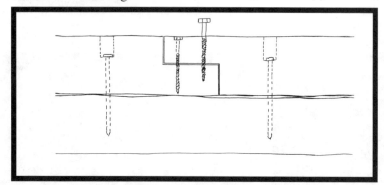

The drawing (above) illustrates how I put he splice together. Photo (upper, R) shows not only the splice but also how logs at the splice itself had to be shimmed. (Lower, R) Splice, chinked & caulked.

Laying One Log Three Times

Laying logs in the manner that I show here I felt later to be a waste of time. The thing was long enough to have covered the entire wall in one piece ... and thick enough with no great taper to worry about. So why was I to lay it three times? Dunno! But I did. And not just this once ... this is the only time that I let you catch me. Watch.

I begin by notching and laying one end in place. The whole is then supported by a chain from a bi-pod whose pointed ends are secured by driving in the ground. I then cut just long enough for the length needed ... now the weight of the remainder is held by the bi-pod. Using the come-a-long, I ease the log further in the desired direction ... support this middle section with 12" spikes, cut again, and come-a-long it the rest of the way. The bottom right photo shows this log, the second down on the

back wall. Note by studying this shot that this wasn't the first time I did it. Duh! I suppose that if the logs tapered a lot and length was a problem that this would be beneficial ... which I suppose is why I include it here. Laying the log as one piece and shimming prior to cutting the openings is much more time efficient.

2nd Story floor joists

For as little as I have drawings and photos to illustrate, this step took a lot of time and effort.

I kept one end of the 2nd story open so as to allow movement of air and people. The small size of the place eliminated any stairwell space. I will eventually build a straight up and down ladder for the inside and a deck on the outside with a regular staircase ... I did put in a door for access to a deck.

I placed a large diameter log (average 10") to run the full 14 foot length (with a temporary middle support until the beam dries out enough to eliminate the chance of any sagging). For the 16' span I used two smaller logs that are spliced into the larger beam ... they are permanently supported at the middle by the main purlin so can be a smaller diameter since they span only 8 feet each.

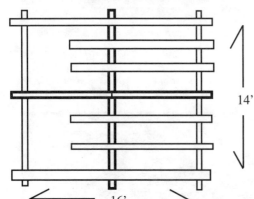

14'

16'

These two supports crossing lengthwise thru the middle of the building serve another purpose in also holding the building together as they are now notched and integrated into the whole. Any tendency of the walls to want to bow in or out are now eliminated.

From one (the south) wall, I now set in logs crossing to the main beam, notching them in carefully as any air space is not support and may lead to sagging. Gaps were later filled with cement so as to create one whole.

I put two beams on each side of the center one giving me an expanse of approximately 32 inches between centers of each beam. Since each

The main beam (spanning 14 feet) is thick enough to support the entire weight when it dries out. Until then I'll keep a brace under it. The other cross piece is supported at the center by the main beam and so doesn't need be as stout (R). Straightness ain't critical (obviously) as you'll only need see the beams when screwing in the floor boards.

beam is approx. 6 inches wide, there is about 26 inches of air for floor boards to cover. Lining the six beams level to the one center cross piece taxed me some. Was tedious. What I did was to set them in just a tad high and then level them off with the chain saw floating the surface. I leveled out from the center, one beam at a time, using a straight piece of 2x4 with a level on it. Worked! Of course from the time that they were set in and the building having weathered thru the winter and spring until the roof was put on the following fall, some settling/twisting/shrinkage/warpage certainly took place.

I sawed boards from logs that I cut late in the season (and the bark was stuck to) for the flooring. Took my time. Maybe one log, two boards, a week. (This will be covered next). I cut them thick for extra strength. I wanted close to a full two inches and got it plus or minus. I put the boards in place as I cut them. This was also time consuming as each had to be individually fitted. I had to keep reminding myself that it was only a log cabin. My leveling certainly wasn't right on and the boards were far from it. I shimmed under each as needed from beam to beam and then, before screwing them in place, ran the chain saw between the two side by side boards to get as good a fit as possible. By the time I went thru the eight I had on hand, most of the floor was done. Later, one log alone gave me five boards that finished it out, which I did after the roof was on. It was easier to do the fitting when the floor was the roof, but those boards weathered to a gray color where the last five pieces keep their rich red cedar color.

The boards may be wavy (R) but they'll do the job. I smoothed the seams so as not to have much to trip over, especially while I was using it as a scaffolding (above) while laying the upper story logs.

Ripping Boards from Logs

Ripping logs into boards may seem daunting at first, but it ain't that bad. There are more efficient ways to cut lumber but not that I am aware of "straight from the saw". The main thing is to have a sharp chain ALWAYS! The sharpness will allow the saw to do the work and all you need do is concentrate on following the guide string.

I ran a string tight from one end of the log to the other, not allowing it to come into contact with the log at any place as this could make it get off straight. After raising at least one end of the log off the ground, I began the cut

(Above) The line following the center cut is run for the left hand cut. The right cut was made first, from the same direction, just using different guide marks on the saw. I made all cuts from the same direction as I felt that the cut might waver more if I made changes ... I wanted as much in my favor as possible.

Note string in relation to saw from my cutting viewpoint (R) ... I kept it in the same position at top of hand guard and at back of saw the entire cut ... also looking back down through the kerf of what I had just cut. When all was in align, the finished board was some-what on the money.

69

about six inches in. Keeping it together at the ends until you're entirely finished makes it easier to keep the log in place as you continue to cut boards ... nothing flopping around. My first cut is to remove the outside round. Then the string was strung again for each additional cut. From the average log, I got two half rounds from the outside and two boards. When the board is trimmed so that there is a straight edge, there will be less flat on the *out* side of the board. I

made certain to keep enough flat on the out side (which I placed *down* on the floor) to help keep the board stabilized when put in place ... not rocking.
 When sawing, the trick is to concentrate and watch carefully the position of the saw. I "marked" two spots off of the saw, one at the front and the other at the rear, and kept the string in line with these as I cut. To do this successfully I made certain that my head was at the same position or else the line could easily get off. I did this by keeping a *visual of the open kerf* that the saw left behind. So ... **1/** from the eye, **2/** thru two points of the saw to the string and **3/** also to the open kerf behind. Enough to concentrate on without having to fight a dull saw. Keep it sharp. I sharpened after each board cut and sometimes more often ... anytime that I felt that I was losing concentration to the saw.

This great log was 30 feet long and was intended for use as a purlin ... which I didn't use. Where I was used to getting 2 boards from a log, this gave me five ... one a full 10" wide by 2" thick. Here (top) I have trimmed my first board and flattened three sides of the log which now makes easier guiding when slicing off additional boards (lower, L-R).

Gables

When the roof line is met at the sides, something needs to be done to finish off the ends. I've seen in many log buildings, both old and new, where the gables are built up using conventional lumber and siding ... and I wonder why? Is there some benefit? I don't know. Anyhow, in my *vast* experience of erecting two log buildings, I felt that the best was to just continue up with logs.

The top log on the sides not gabled (huh?) have to be pretty good ones ... the roof will set on these. Take extra care with these to insure that they are right at level and run smooth as much as possible (remember, it's just a log cabin)

Care has to be taken to insure that the log just don't roll off ... remember, no side walls to hold them. This and getting the logs up there are the two major differences that I came across. Let's check 'em out.

I elected to off set the roof line at the last moment ... therefore the extra purlin for boards. This allowed me to raise one side wall higher than the other (for the salt box shape) and

let me have the benefit of at least having one end tied to a secure wall for two more courses. When I began to set one of the ends free (not tied to the wall) I raised a handy log like a flag pole and tied it in to the building, once high up and once lower down, so that the logs would have something semi-secure to rest against in the outward direction at least. I then ran a rope from the projected finished height (from the pole) off to the roof level to guide how long (short) each additional log need be.

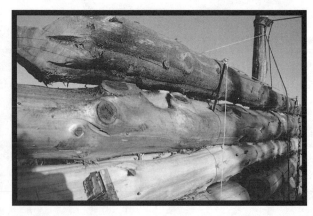

(Clockwise from above) Once I got the log up and in place (next chapter) I then had the problem of keeping it there while I did all the leveling, plumbing and spiking. What I came up with was setting spikes at intervals ... at least one at each end ... angled out from the log below ... like a cradle. This allowed me to roll the log I was working on in whatever direction without fear of losing it to gravity. When I had it in the position that suited me, I just used a piece of cord and tied opposing spikes together tightly to bind the log in place while I countersunk holes and set in spikes. Then I raised another.

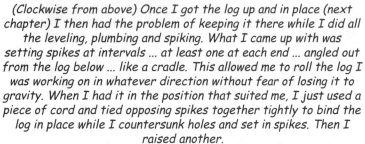

Misplaced Spikes

I t's a real pain to hafta redo spikes. Try to get 'em where you want 'em (& not where you don't) as you go. But as careful as you are (at least me) I ran across the misplaced spike. Sometimes with the saw ... oops! In this series of photos, I show what happened when I misread the line I had running from the projected roof top to the side walls (three pages back). This had to be cut later to fit the roof ... and guess what I found? (Actually I had marked the position of these spikes with a pencil and was able to find this without hurting the saw.)

I first cut close with the saw and then got to it using a hatchet. When I cut under and around it, I could have pulled it if I wished but since the lower portion was out of the line, I just set it in deeper using the shown angled piece of metal (gate hinge) as a countersink.

Chapter 11

Raising &
Moving Logs

Moving these heavy logs around requires more than just brute strength and fortunately there are methods and devices available to enable us to do so.

For the most part cables, rope and pulleys of a sort are all that is needed. To pull a log up a hill that you can't run a straight line to can be done simply by snaking a rope or cable thru the trees ... but this is hard on the puller and the pulling equipment. Placing diversions in route thru which you can run the cable eases this chore lots. Everytime the cable were to run *around* a tree, instead attach a "D" ring, pulley, etc. in *front* of and to the tree and run the rope thru it. Much smoother.

I have raised logs that had fallen below high banks simple by placing an in-line diversion such as this above it and so that the pull would run upwards. This was the more common way that I raised logs to the second story of the building.

Let's let the photos talk for a while.

Lifting #1

Since we just finished working on gables, let's show how I got some of those logs up there. I used this technique only a coupla times. The upright has to be a solid pole or it can break. I ran a cable thru a carabiner (D ring) attached to the upright and this was run off to the winch. It would have been stronger if in fact I ran the cable back down again from the first carabiner (or snatch block) at the top to another below and then off to the winch as then the force would have been downward on the pole.
I attached a chain to each end of the log to be raised, found the center of gravity and hooked there. The log raised perfectly as shown.

Lifting #2

This is the method that I used to get most of the logs to the height of about the loft floor. It's based loosely on a device known as a gin pole which I read about sometime in the past ... but couldn't for the life of me find anything about when I wanted it.

Here a bi-pod is the main support, two logs pointed at the bottom and chained securely at the top. The base was driven into the ground. A long arm (log) was laid into the crotch of the bi-pod. Now the rule of the fulcrum shown is that a little bit of the arm is left sticking out the lifting side ... a lot on the other. I held the long arm as high as I could (here in the step of a ladder) and ran a chain from the short arm to the log to be raised. The further out the chain on the end, the more it raised the log but also the more weight that was needed to raise it. The set up I ended with used its own weight to pull it and hold it. After each lift, the log was set on a block, chain removed and all was re-peated. I raised the log to a convenient working height and notched it before raising it all the way up. When in position, the bi-pod/chain held the loose end while I made adjustments to the notch. The notch held the log securely while I set the spikes.

Lifting #3

A variation of the last method. Instead of a lifting arm, I used the come-a-long. In reality you'll probably find yourself using a combination of many of these and others that only you and your particular situation will come up with.

Lifting #4

Well, I'm not real sure what I was doing here. It appears that I got the left side as high as I could using the come-a-long and bi-pod and am in the process of raising the right side by the same method. But ... I kinda got myself stuck. Unless there is an arm extending beyond the notched ends of the wall, the raising log gets bound by them.

It's **very dangerous**
to work under a piece such as this trying to free it with a bar ...
don't ever do it.

Never place yourself in a position that can hurt or kill you if a piece of equipment fails!

I eventually ended taking the bi-pod on to the outside and running the left end of the log between it and the wall.
It worked ...
but it used a lot of time and effort.

Lifting #5

*T*he method of raising logs shown here is maybe one of the oldest and more commonly used that I'm aware of. Been around for a long time. There are so many points of contact reducing weight/pull made by the cable that it seems almost effortless to move a large log up the ramp. The cable is run from a tie off point on either side, around the ends of the log and back to a central point where a pulley or snatch block is attached. The pull originates from here using winch or come-a-long.

One end of the log being larger in diameter than the other makes for one side to raise faster ... and it is wise to lift the lower end on occasion so that not too much weight overloads any one side, maybe causing a slipping out of the log. Geri has lifted the one end with no apparent effort.

Just don't get under it!
You'll see this in action in about another 20 pages.

Direction
of pull

Lifting
#6

I saved my favorite for last.

As with choosing quality logs in the field, I suppose that finding the most convenient and easy way to raise logs comes with experience. I began using this method during the second year of building when I had gotten into the upper floor, but the same would work as well at the lower levels.

First move one end of the log, preferably the larger one, to the base of the wall, keeping the log as *parallel to the wall* as possible. Before raising, trim the end so that no pointy things are sticking out to catch as it rubs against the walls during the raising procedure. The cable is run over the top log of the wall and down to the log where a chain is fastened as close to the end as is safe ... close to the end to keep the *angle of pull as straight up* as possible and yet secure enough not to slip free.

A loose 300 to 500 pound log can create havoc. Be safety conscious!

The cable is adjusted by diversions (note photos).

Pulling the log to the wall.

80

You can pull from any direction and yet keep the cable pulling straight up. Once you are in the working mode and have various chains, snatch blocks, and carabiners handy, all this falls in place pretty smoothly.

Raise the end of the log as far as it wants to go. There may be a few times that it does catch against the wall, so go slow ... don't want to snap a cable or anything. If tension is felt, check it out before proceeding. Most times a simple prying with a bar (from above) will free it. Once at the top it will usually require a few trips from winch or come-a-long to the point where the end is fighting its way over the top log. Don't rush. Put a bit of tension, then pry. Repeat as necessary until the end is *on* the top. At some point during this last stage swing the other end of the log out until it's at a 90° angle to the wall.

Once the end of the log is securely resting on the top of the wall and the other end is swung out so that the log is now at a 90° angle, slowly release the tension. Make sure that it wants to stay put. Then slide the chain down the log several feet, keeping the hook of the cable as close to the log as possible so that it doesn't require attention every time it moves over the top of the wall. If the chain is kept hooked to the end of the log which is now beyond and above the wall, there is too much effort required to pull because you are actually pulling the top of the log down and the bottom up at the same time ... trying to bend it. If you have a **straight line of pull** from where the **cable diverts** (on the back wall?) over the **top of the working wall** to the **chain hooked lower on the log**, *it will pull straight and smoothly*. But!

When enough weight is put forward on the log (becomes top heavy), it may want to fall to one side or the other. I prepare for this by tying a rope off from the end of the log to both sides. The rope I keep loose enough to allow the log to pull free but also tight enough to keep the log from falling too far uncontrollably.

At a certain "magic moment", the log will balance. Neat! Just be prepared for it to continue its lowering at the pulled end. Unless the log is extremely long, when it does fall into the building, it won't reach the other wall. I kept a 6 inch diameter log up there for just this purpose. It reached from wall to wall in either direction and was easy to move simply by rolling around the top of the walls. I could conveniently put it wherever I wanted to. With either the winch or come-a-long, I would just ease the log forward slowly until is gently lowered itself. Simple? Yeah.

Again, moving it around when you finally get it spanning the walls is a simple matter. Sometimes maybe too much so ... when a *true* log gets to rolling, maybe it won't want to stop. Be prepared for this. When rolling ends near to corners, or other times when it might fall free if not stopped, back up your work with a chain. You do not want to lose control ... it could be disastrous.

Raising the blunted end ...
not a big deal.
Be careful and go slow.
Note log is parallel to wall above
and at 90° angle at right.

Move the base of the log to a 90° angle to the wall for more controlled pulling over the top.

When the end is above the wall, tie it off loosely with a rope to keep it from falling off to the side.

Chain is run down log about 1/3 the distance in photo above and has been moved close to the bottom in photo at right, where the log is just about balanced.

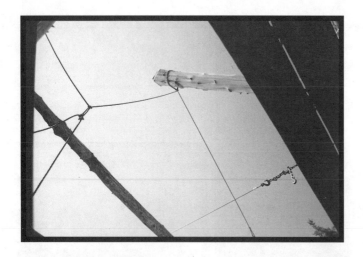

(Clockwise from upper left) 1/ Rope guides log as winch pulls, 2/ log balances and 3/ falls gently onto waiting cross log. A long log 4/ leaves a lot sticking outside to be cut off later.

Line of Pull

(Top, l to R) From winch, over wall, thru snatch block and carabiner ... a smooth line of pull. As viewed from above (below left). Always back up your rolling logs with a safety chain (below R).

Chapter 12

Preparing For The Roof

Up to now what we've been doing is cutting and laying logs ... along with a few hundred other things that have needed be done also. We have a pile of logs that are well held together ... it'll keep horses or corn in but not rain or wind out. We now are at a major milestone ... we begin to make it a house!

Before we can begin to put up a roof tho, we have a bit of preparation. The top logs on the <u>side</u> walls should be some of your better ones. The roof will be nailed directly to these. In what we built here, one side wall was built two logs higher than the other. I gabled up from these to what I determined was to be the actual top of the roof. No plans here. I made most all of these decisions as I went ... started building and let the logs fall where they may. At the last minute I decided to offset the roof line because, well, just because, I guess. Well, maybe it's a bit more than that. Let me try to explain how my mind was working.

• The second story floor ran only about 3/4th the way across

I gotta now make the ragged roof line suitable for a roof.

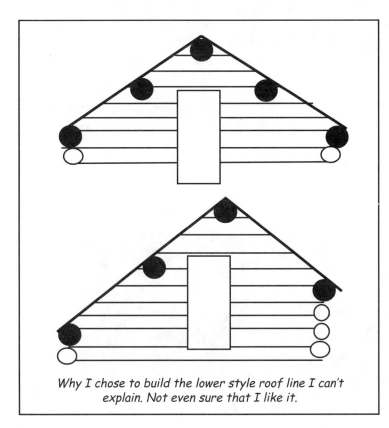

Why I chose to build the lower style roof line I can't explain. Not even sure that I like it.

the house, another determination that I made at the time I approached it during construction (I kinda envisioned standing at the edge of the floor (balcony?), leaning on a rail and visiting with folks sitting around the stove below). I coulda had the floor cross the entire distance but felt that that would make me feel more crowded. Isolated. I could still enclose the floor if I want to.

• Once that the floor plan was determined and the walls were a coupla feet above its level, I could more readily see what was about to be. The shorter wall could be a great place for a large, unopening, window. A wonderful source of light ... for both upstairs and down.

• At this stage I stood where the upstair's door was to be (openings were already left in the logs so I couldn't change its position) and picked the spot where the top of the door needed to be.

The upright pole support for the outside of the gable was in place. I chose a spot of minimum height for this mark (top of door plus distance for a solid one piece log header for support above the door ... room for a coupla logs above as the gable roof line would be slanted), and

marked. I determined this mark on the opposing wall (thru leveling tricks shown before), marked, and ran a rope as a guide between. This rope served another purpose besides as a mark of where I wanted the bottom of the top purlin to be ... it also helped to steady the two gables by pulling in against the stress of the upright poles.

• I had no shortage of logs on hand ... in fact I had on hand all that I needed to finish the building ... including more than enough logs good enough to be used for purlins. There were (and are) several still standing in the timber.

• If I centered the roof line, the gable logs would not be more in number but it looked like maybe more in length as the taper would be shallower on each side (?). I don't know.

Whatever reasoning, I chose to build the roof off center ... and I'm not certain yet that I like it. So it goes.

So how we gonna go about it?

The ragged line of logs as they appeared as I raised my top purlin ... something that changed for the second one.

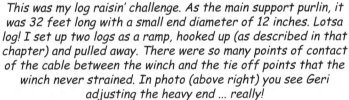

This was my log raisin' challenge. As the main support purlin, it was 32 feet long with a small end diameter of 12 inches. Lotsa log! I set up two logs as a ramp, hooked up (as described in that chapter) and pulled away. There were so many points of contact of the cable between the winch and the tie off points that the winch never strained. In photo (above right) you see Geri adjusting the heavy end ... really!

The lower right photo shows that something has to give ... the log is about to run into the tree. I placed a ladder against the tree and cut about two feet off (which I guess will make a neat stool) ... don't know what to tell you I'da done if the tree wasn't there. Ladder against the log, ten feet in the air and me with a running chain saw? (Duh! Wouldn't need to cut it
<u>if tree wasn't there</u> ... Geri caught this.)

This is a smooth way to bring the logs up and safe if all rules are followed ... #1 of which is to

never place yourself under the log in the event that something does fail.

Log to the top of the ramp (above) and now to move it up, over the log ends, into position at the very peak. Do take note of the position of the top of the ramp log (right, in photo at upper right). The end of it is placed such that the upcoming log is free to roll off of it and onto the cabin with no obstacles.

Well, the bar and brute strength will do just so much, especially for a little guy. So after struggling with it for just so long (upper right) I think, "wonder what'd happen if I smoothed the angle? (lower right) ... Duh!

I then worked an end up over each log, one at a time, one end and then the other. I didn't want to go too high on either end and have the slightest chance that the log might wanna slide off. While working one end, the other was _always_ secured in place with chain, spike or both to prevent it from falling loose.

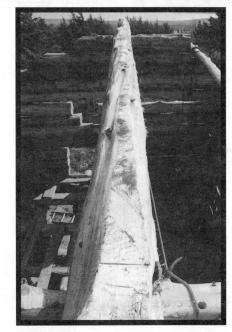

I cut the rough notch to receive the purlin prior to bringing it up. Once the purlin has been wrestled to the top I made more refined adjustments to the notch ... I wanted to mess putting it in place as little as possible ... remember, I'm perched however, 14' from the ground, working with this pretty heavy log end and chain saw. I got tingles.

I had taken the measurements of the thickness of the log ends, measured down from my leveled rope guide (remember that?), marked into the top log and cut. Must've done something right because I had only to lift out an end and make adjustments once. Before spiking the purlin to the walls, make certain that the gable ends are straight up and down ... they could have gotten off plumb with all the wrestlin' around. When the walls are plumb and the purlin is positioned to give you the overhang that you want (four feet per side for this) and the purlin is level, set the spikes.

Once in place, the top line of the log straight (or as can be for a log), the level level when placed on it at various intervals, I stood on top at one end and cheered my accomplishment ... for about ten seconds (took the photo, lower right) ... the tingling won out and I went back to work.

Now for the second purlin. Maybe not quite as massive as the first, but when I'm working with such massive logs, I can't tell 100# one way or the other.

Now that I had a firm upper mark (the top of the purlin), I ran a string (top left) from it to the top of the last log on the side wall and marked a line ... the plane that the roof will be. I then made my first cut (top right) taking care to not cut below the line ... followed by a check with the level (left) and a finish cut (lower left) to give a smooth roof line.

Before I hauled the second purlin up, I had to have things ready since I had cut the roof line and I didn't have a platform to securely hold it while working. I studied the rounded shaped of the purlin at the point that they were to make contact with the walls (four feet in from each end), found the position of them on the wall (one half the space from the top to the bottom) and sketched rough openings (upper, right). I did my best to make these cuts right, or even just a tad larger, as it would be more trouble to remove them and make adjustments (two middle photos). They fit! (Bottom photos) All of the purlins are longer than the building is ... in this case four feet at both ends. I want my roof to extend well beyond the walls to offer protection from both the moisture and the sun.

93

Hey! ... I was just so tickled to be at this point, I
took a lot of photos ... and of course,
I gotta share some with you.

Chapter 13

Building the Roof

Now is the true test of just how well the basic rules of level and plumb have been followed in our building project. Not that it really matters for most of us in a project such as this ... but the closer to true, the stronger the whole. If the line of shingles wavers and weaves and the two ends don't match up? ... so be it. Most who visit and/or spend the night in this probably wouldn't know what to look for anyhow. If they say something snide about the rows of shingles not looking so good, well, send 'em on their way.

OK. Remember how we found square way back when we were preparing the foundation? ... let's do it again. Go to the junction of main purlin and the wall, look down the line of log ends of the wall, judge their center and put a nail on top of the purlin. Put another nail at the center of the bottom log face (the

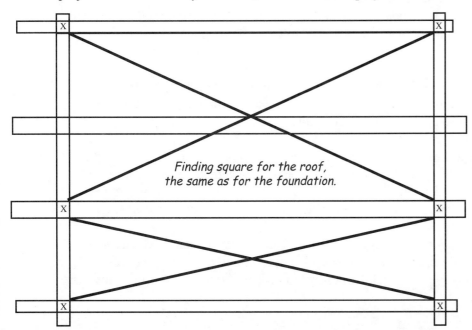

*Finding square for the roof,
the same as for the foundation.*

ones we cut slanted) lower down at the junction of the two walls. Do you follow me? I'll try once again. Like, from a distance you're looking at the side of the building, placing the slant cut gable logs in a straight line. You want a nail at the bottom of the gable logs, at the junction of the walls, in the center. You also want a nail in this same line of sight at the top of this line, on top of the main purlin.

Repeat for the other end. You now have four nails ... one at each corner of the roof at the center of the log junctions.

Now ... we want the distance from nails on the purlins to the nails on the walls to be equal 10 1/2 feet on one side, 10 1/2 on the other. Same measuring the other way ... 14 feet one way, 14 the other.

So now if you set this all up and have been real good about your building procedures, the distance diagonally will be somewhere close (remember, just a log cabin). In our case, we were within less than an inch! I was surprised, but pleased.

Repeat this for the other side of the roof.

The purpose of this is not a test. It is what it is. But when I got to laying the ceiling boards (2x6 & 2x8's) I wanted to know how much I might need to adjust them from square/straight. If I was several inches off, I would like to have adjusted maybe a coupla inches per side so that it wouldn't look quite so bad. If you're using 4x8 sheets of plywood, the seams may not be as noticeable.

So just what is the roof? We have two purlins, two top logs at the sides and two gables at the end ... all pretty much in line and at the same level. We gotta get it covered. The most basic could be something as simple as sheets of plywood (the plywood could be intermixed with old boards), cut to fit and covered with tarpaper. That would work. Just something solid enough to walk on and waterproof to keep out the rain. The steeper the slope, the less strong needs be the roofing as the weight will want to slide off.

I wanted just a coupla steps up from this. For looks, (**1**) boards for the ceiling (inside facing) which also acted as strength. 2x's served this purpose. I could have stopped there and just laid tarpaper, but! ... again, I wanted a bit more. On top of the boards I put down a layer of (**2**) roofing felt (light weight tarpaper) ... the only function of which was to hide the color of the next layer (pink) which could be seen thru the cracks between the boards. To help retain the heat (during the winter, keep it out during the summer) I laid sheets of (**3**) insulation as my next layer. These come in various thicknesses, I used the minimum of 1/2 inch. Even this much keeps frost on the roof when there is a fire on the inside all day long. Walking around on these sheets would hurt them so on to this was laid sheets of scrap (**4**) 1/2 inch plywood and wafer board that we picked up at sales. This *sheathing* not only added protection for the insulation, but also added just a bit of its own insulation. It also provides something for nails to dig into when putting down shingles. On top of the plywood was put another (**5**) layer of felt (two is better ... it's inexpensive). And to literally top it off comes the (**6**) shingles. This

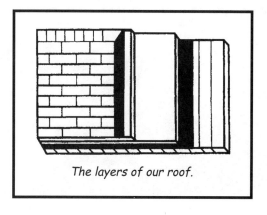

The layers of our roof.

keeps out the rain. Rolled roofing or tarpaper could have been used but really doesn't save that much ... either in $ or time.

Now let's take it step by step.

Nailing on of the ceiling boards. Here is where most of the dollars went that we spent on this cabin. In the year prior to getting to this stage I had attended several farm sales where lumber was up for bid. I turned most of it down because I was foolish ... or fussy. I wanted the facing boards of our ceiling to as light in color as possible ... and to me that meant new. I didn't relish having the gray color of weathered boards, not because I have anything against *used* or *gray*, I just wanted to reflect as much light as possible. If I had been aware of the price of new lumber, I might have changed my mind. But!

I bought 2x6's and 2x8's because I felt that the slight variance of sizes might be more, what, rustic? (then why not gray?). So on we go. I used the nails at one end of the roof line as my guide for placing in the first board. Remember, if this one is off kilter, they all will be. Since this board was placed on top of the gable logs, there was some

Ceiling Boards

gapping underneath where things didn't meet quite perfectly. I placed under this first board a strip of foam called "sill seal", which is compressed when the board is nailed in placed to create a tight seal. But this became so much bother (kept slipping out) that I only used it in the one spot ... and filled the rest with caulking later during finishing. Since the nails were placed properly to start the boards on line, the only thing to keep an eye on as I went as far as alignment is concerned, was to keep the ends of the boards semi straight. I did this by running a string along the top of the purlin and bringing the boards to it, thereby everything ended as smooth and square as was possible under the circumstances.

Lined up. (Above) First board set in place at one end (both sides) and guide string run down center of main purlin (left).

Once the building itself was covered, I laid the boards out to my mark (four feet, more or less) on the overhanging purlins. Since I was using a mixture of sizes with the 2x's, when I got to the end of the second side of the roof, things didn't quite line up. Out with the fix anything chain saw. A line was run and off it came. After doubling all checks to insure no mistakes were to be made, the purlins were trimmed to the boards.

Hey! ... a roof, almost.

Nails to guide the first board placement ... a third one set <u>between</u> the two "squaring" nails.

Placing a seal under the boards at the gables is a good idea (upper L) tho any gaps (upper R) can be filled in later with caulking. The boards will run from top purlin, over the middle purlin to sit on the top of the wall. All these points, along with the gable ends, need be somewhat in line. Photo (lower, L) needs be looked at carefully to see the middle purlin just below the line of the wall log ... a gable log visible on left side. Photo (middle, R) shows a bump (knot) in purlin which needs be removed (lower, R) for smooth transition of the board, tho the board will bend to flow over slight dips and bumps. Addition roofing layers will smooth this even further.

(Left) Nailing boards in place ... 3 nails per contact point ... one straight in, two at angles. Using coated nails, these boards should never come undone.

When I reached the end of the Purlins (Left, & 2 below), one layer was wider. A chain saw made short work of that. (Right) The finished line. The crook that shows here doesn't really exist ... trick photography, really. The camera was slightly off centered and so it only appears "not straight".

(Above) Finished ceiling from inside.

We got one more step before we're finished with this portion of the job. Mostly because the logs are imperfect, the ends sticking out overhanging the wall are, how to say it, not neat. Things will not only look better, but the work will be easier from here out if we correct it. I took straight 2x4's, clamped them in place at the edge of the boards and screwed them in solidly. Never having faced a problem like this before, I was somewhat happily surprised at just how well this worked. Any fringe elements hanging out were then trimmed with the trusty, do all, chain saw.

Insulation & Sheathing

Ceiling boards in place, covered with felt. Next step, insulation. Putting these lightweight sheets in place in any sort of wind can be a challenge ... big, expensive kites. If there's no wind the job ain't bad. You gotta line corners and sides up ... but anything that sticks out can easily be cut off. A helper helps here. Just a coupla nails per sheet will hold them but a few more is safer if wind is a possibility. Where the two sides meet at the top purlin center line, just have one butt into the other. This will go fast. Lotsa ladders and a helper plus maybe a safety rope come in handy. Its best to do this and the next layer at the same time so that the insulation isn't left exposed to possible wind damage.

Follow with the sheathing ... sheets of plywood. 1/2 inch is the standard for this job (I think), lighter weight material will work here because of solid, direct contact with the rest of the roof ... thicker, 3/4", is a waste of dollars if lighter weight is available. Use what you got. It's only a log cabin. I had picked up several sheets of 1/2" wafer (or press) board at a farm sale cheap. I had a coupla sheets of 1/2" plywood laying around from other projects. I think I had to buy maybe four. As with the insulation sheets, have them square and in line at corners and edges. The chain saw can take care of any overhanging trouble spots. Try to keep seams of the two layers from lining up.

Once you got this all taken care of, a layer (two is better) of roofing felt is then stapled on. Overlap this layer by at least six inches ... rolls are marked. Begin at the bottom, following in sequence by other layers *on top* as you go up ... this allows any moisture to flow *over* rather than *under*. Walking on this surface can be enlightening. Don't! The paper can slip on the layer below and ... **Whooooops!** Trim the felt at the edge all the way around so the wind don't catch it. Leave just a little overhanging for now.

A facing board can be put on now. Don't suppose that it's really absolutely necessary but it looks better and does control moisture from getting in under these other layers. Not expensive or hard to do. So you might's well.

Now, onto this we add one last thing ... drip plate and edging. Edging to the sides and the drip plate to the bottoms, these galvanized metal strips encourage the water to flow off of and away from the board facing. Also inexpensive, it's good insurance ... quick and easy to install.

Y'almost gotta roof.

Lotsa ladders (R) makes it easier and safer when working around up there, even, and especially, for two. Where the two sides meet at the peak, it's a simple matter to trim it evenly with the chain saw. Keep this area (L) kinda neat, even filling openings and cracks with scraps of insulation, rolled felt or strips of plywood. The only protection over this are the shingles.

Face Board

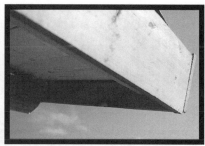

Putting up of the facing board is easy enough and good insurance against rain getting under the roof and maybe starting things to rot. Careful cutting and matching of the corners ain't too critical (above). Front boards meeting at the apex (left) require a bit more attention. Here I simply used a level to give me a straight up & down line & then cut off with a ... hand saw. Yep, I do have one. Any gap can be filled with caulking if so desired.

Drip Plate

L aying in drip edge is easy ... put on roof trim board, _under_ felt. I always put goop (roofing cement) along the edge under the edge strip, nail it in place, goop again on top and cover with felt. If not already, trim the felt to about as shown.

With the completion of this step, we're almost done with the roof. Plan on one day to place the ceiling boards in place (if all goes well) and another to get to here. Whenever you leave the felt for any period of time (or when working in any wind) it's the best to secure all edges with scrap lumber nailed down to keep it all from blowing away (above). The roof now looks almost complete, neat edges and all (below).

Shingling

Alright!

The final step to finishing the roof, shingling is really a simple and fun job ... most especially if you have ended with a pretty much square roof. Every package of shingles that I have ever bought has had good instructions on how to put them in place. I'll do my best to explain it some here.

A shingle has three flaps... kinda like three shingles in one. Every other row of shingles put in place has one of these sections removed so that the line staggers from row to row. The first row is actually two shingles thick. Cut off the lower portion of however many shingles that it takes to cover one row and nail it in place (as per instructions on package), the bottom of which is to stick out just a tad beyond the metal edging. The ends also are to be placed so as to hang about 3/8th of an inch over the edge. The second layer, with the flappy cut off, is laid to line up with the bottom edge of the first. If the roof line is pretty much on, then a string can be used to insure that the shingles are in a straight line. If the edge wavers a bit much, then lay this second course to align with the first and use a string to straighten the row of the next course where it won't be quite as noticeable. (Huh?). Then simply repeat ... until you reach the peak. Don't forget to cut a flappy off every other row.

When one side reaches the peak, go as high as allowed (see photo's) and bend the upper portion over ... this adds just a little mass to the peak. Shingle up the other side and flap over as before. Almost done.

Now you gotta peak it all off with a ridge cap ... again explained in detail on bundles of shingles. Take a razor knife and cut a bunch of shingle into thirds (note photo) ... then trim (not mandatory, but is neater). Nail these cut pieces along as shown, overlapping the one prior by about 5 inches.

When finished ... **You gotta roof!!!**

The first coupla courses of shingles is best done from a ladder ... the steeper the roof, the more important this is (below).

First course of shingles should stick out at bottom and ends just a bit, Use lots of roof cement under the first course and all the way up on the sides. Run a string every five rows or so to insure that the line of shingles stays straight.

Chimney

*T*he easiest time to put holes in the roof (for chimneys, etc.) is when laying shingles. If done after, there is more of a hassle lifting and redoing shingles. I, of course, chose the easy route ... here showing the installation of the chimney.

After determining where to make the hole from the inside, I built a support (top, L), drilled holes (from inside to out) to mark the corners so as to clear the area of any obstacles and then I cut the opening (chain saw).

A chimney support box was then leveled and nailed into position

Insulated chimney pipe is then placed in the box (upper, L). Flashing is then marked where it will sit, lotsa goop (roofing cement) applied (upper, R) and the flashing then set permanently with nails (lower, L). Goop is then run around the flashing, insuring to cover all nails (lower, middle), and shingling is continued. Note that the top of the flashing is under shingles and that the lower portion of the flashing is on top of the shingles. Water then has no means to flow <u>under</u>, becoming a leak.

Ridgecap

Putting on the ridge cap ... a nice place to be.
A whole lot of work behind us.
Remember when we laid boards, insulation and plywood
... some rough gaps at the peak. The reason that we
wanted to kinda firm them up some, if even only with
rolled & crumpled roofing felt, was because the only
thing at the peak is a few layers of shingles. If'n
whenever we happened to step on this, it could crush
and break the shingles thereby causing leaking.
First side to the peak is just laid over ... then the
second over it (two layers now). A coupla more are
added when we do the ridge cap itself.
Feels real good about now!

Roofed!

Chapter 14

Putting in Windows & Doors

Now that we have a roof, we gotta do something about the doors and windows. I'll here go step by step on how to set one window in.

You have to make the hole in the wall larger than the window. My "blueprints" I just kinda scratched out for each opening as I went on whatever scrap paper or board was available. If the inside of the window, the part that fits into the opening, is, lets say, 30" by 40 ", that's your starting point. You figure *out* from there. I like things to fit kinda snug and leave only 1/2" total *extra* for the sides. Up & down I leave more as there needs to be extra space at the top. Logs will settle and this needs to be taken into account. I left a minimum of one inch above the door and window frames ... none *required* that much.

We are putting these logs in green. As I mentioned before, Eastern Red Cedar will shrink

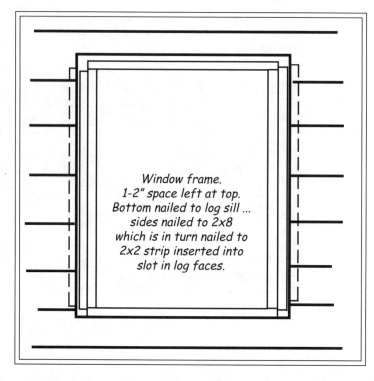

Window frame.
1-2" space left at top.
Bottom nailed to log sill ...
sides nailed to 2x8
which is in turn nailed to
2x2 strip inserted into
slot in log faces.

only 1%. That's one inch per 100 ... and measuring from top to bottom of window & door openings, the space devoted to concrete can be subtracted as that will not shrink. All the space above and below the opening you can just forget about here. The shrinkage of those has no relationship on our openings as the shrinkage is *within* *only* *their* *planes*. The roof will settle the entire distance shrunk ... the openings only by what is beside them. Kinda get that?

For this example, take 30x40 inches. At each side I want two 2x8 inch boards ... at 1 1/2 inch apiece (don't know how they get 1 1/2 inches outta 2 ... but mine ain't to reason why) ... that gives us 3 inches per side for a total of 36 1/2 inches (including the extra 1/2 inch that I need) that needs to removed. Height, 40". I put one 2x8 on the bottom of the frame and one at the top (you'll understand this more thru the photo's and drawing). That makes for an additional 3 inches, plus the one inch extra at the top for settling (I usually left two or more inches as insurance).

The logs *will* settle. Because of this we don't want to securely fasten the sides of the window frames to the log walls ... it could do damage. What we do here is cut a slot into the wall to fit a smaller piece of lumber, with us it was a 2x2" strip ... in the old time log cabin illustrated earlier and later in this book, a straight limb of a tree was used. This strip should fit snugly ... the frame is nailed to it ... and we don't want the frame to wobble in the wall. What I did throughout with this building was to nail a 2x8 to this strip ... then nail the window frame to this giving two thick-nesses at the sides. Why? Don't really know. In a coupla spots I had room only for one 2x8 and this is most certainly as strong as two. Anyhow, that's how I did it. Probably used too many spikes in laying the logs too. Rather overbuild than under.

Top & bottom got one 2x8 each. The bottom was nailed directly to the log sill ... the top, I guess I figured just wouldn't warp out of shape so much in 30 inches to affect the window. Also remember that an extra 1/2 inch was left at the top. This extra space left at the top and sides is so that the window will fit freely into the opening, allowing you to make minor adjustments for leveling. The window will operate best when it is level.

Opening cut in wall. Slots cut for nailing strips and 2x8 nailed to it. Frame inserted, leveled and nailed to this. The window is now inserted and shimmed until level. Some windows have an outside frame integral to it and this is what is nailed to the face of the framework. Others come without and you must add your own outside facing boards. We got our doors and windows from several sources; a couple new, left over from jobs ... others from farm or garage sales ... some given to us (used) by friends. I took what I could get. Whichever, you just gotta work with what you have.

I built frames for the windows and doors from 1x4 inch lumber (some bad mistakes to cover took 1x6's). This protects moisture from getting in on the and just looks better on the inside. Because of the extra space left above the frames, on the outside I put metal flashing above to enclose it, using lotsa caulking to seal it off from weather and insects. Not being a finishing man, I didn't relish this part as much as the rough log work ... but it's all part of the package. Each one becomes easier as you learn what you're doing.

The window determines the size of the opening... it must be square, level and plumb all the way around. Trimming logs at sides is no biggy, and removing wood from bottom log is not a real chore. Removing from overhead is another whole story. Enough log must be left at top as a header so that nothing bends or sags.

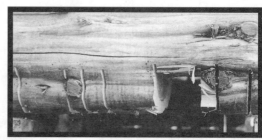

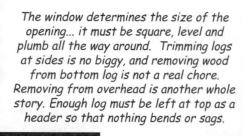

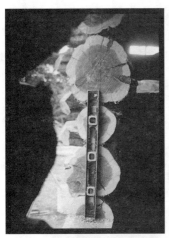

Cutting the slot for the nailer is another chore that I kept wanting to put off ... but once approached wasn't so bad ... just gotta do this stuff. If you weren't up to it, you wouldn't be working so hard for the cabin in the first place.

Find level in the center of the log wall (upper, L). Chain saw is used to line out your pencil marks (either side of the level) ... and then to remove the rest. You even get to sit down for this. This hasta be level! If a spike shows up, a wood chisel is the safest way to remove wood and get it out (right three photos).

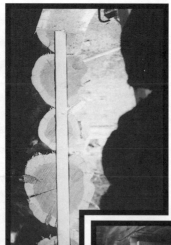

2x2 nailers were ripped from 2x8's with chain saw (above) giving me three per board. Cut to length, a little short to allow for settling, and rounded with hatchet at each end to more match round cut of saw (above right two photo's), the rough cut nailers fit just snugly right into the rough cut slot. **After insuring level,** 2x8" boards were then nailed to the 2x2's.

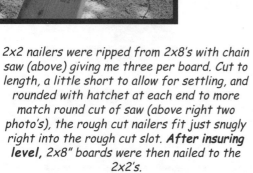

Nail the frame together and fit it into the opening. Level. The facing of the nailers and the frame should be even ... if not make the frame plumb. More important for the window to be so. If any of the nailer boards protrude, cut or rasp 'em even.

At some point the logs have to be beveled (far right) into the same size as the window frames so that the trim fits. Now is as good a time as any. Geri chinks as I paint window trim (R).

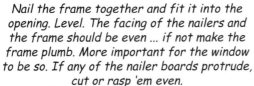

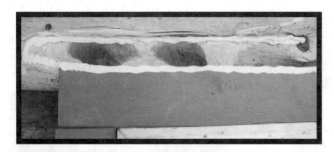

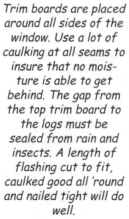

Trim boards are placed around all sides of the window. Use a lot of caulking at all seams to insure that no moisture is able to get behind. The gap from the top trim board to the logs must be sealed from rain and insects. A length of flashing cut to fit, caulked good all 'round and nailed tight will do well.

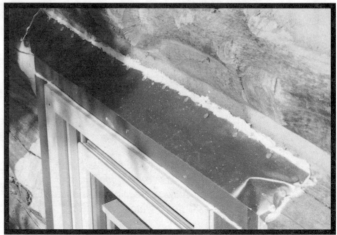

The inside of the window ain't tough to finish off ... more pieces to cut & fit tho. Boards have to be cut & placed all around the inside of the frame ... in some cases this is what prevents the window from coming through. The bottom piece, put in first, is a 2x8" notched to fit in the sill, nailed to the base, and becomes a solid window sill. Logs need be beveled in and trim applied as on the outside for the finished look. For a rough cabin, no finishing is necessary inside.
(Right) Finished windows, inside and

119

Door frames are done the same as windows except that the bottom "sill" should be treated lumber as it will most likely be exposed to the weather. From the space where the door will cover when closed, it's a good idea to also bevel the rest to the outside so that water can roll off. Set it in cement (below, right). We had to put glass in the two we used downstairs (one at upper right). Insure that the hole is square. You need a solid core door for this. Line one side of the opening with trim boards (being cut with skill saw, upper L), level, caulk all around, place in glass, caulk again, and another set of trim boards to hold it. Caulk again at all seams.

The opening (above, left) was cut out of a solid wall of logs. I was offered a sliding glass patio door for free. This is the low side of the house and light from here will benefit up as well as down stairs. With all of the other windows, doors and a vent on the roof, additional ventilation isn't necessary. I took one half of this door and installed it sideways here. As with installing the door window, I simply placed 2x2's around the inside of the frame (leveled and square ... glass don't bend), set in the window and placed more 2x2's on the outside to hold it. All was caulked well.

The opening here is quite a bit larger than what I had intended ... just that the window I got cheap was big. So in it was to go.

Whenever I cut through set logs, I was cautious of spikes ... none encountered here that gave troubles. But when I measured for the rough opening I must've taken a wrong turn ... the window didn't fit. Well, as Harlan used to say, it's not a screw up if you can fix it ... and I did.

To fix, first nails were pulled.
Then chain saw, hatchet and
wood chisel removed about
1/2 inch of wood from one side
and the bottom.
This was one of my latter
windows and if it were one of
the earlier ones, I just mighta
pulled the frame out, rebuilt it
and used the lumber elsewhere
... but I was runnin' outta places
to use scrap pieces.

Sure, it fits now. And who's to know the difference. Note that this window is one that has no outside framework to hold it in place. All I had to do here was nail the 1x4" framework to the window 2x8" framework to keep it from falling forward. A coupla nails lightly tacked thru the inside window frame will hold it in place until I finish the inside trim.

Chapter 15   Cleaning the Ends

The corners of the building where the logs jut out past the notch require special attention. If left as is, with the logs crowded together, any moisture that was to get in would stay ... and rot would become a real issue.

I spent some time going thru each corner with the chain saw, creating gaps enough between so that the air could dry things out, and also shaping and beveling each log end so that rain would run off of each.

Just another one of those tasks that I felt needed to be done to ensure that this building lasted at least as long as I.

(Below) The Cabin with rough shod log ends. A close up of the right hand corner (middle) before and (right) after cutting to length and rounding ends.

That corner is illustrated here a bit closer up. (Left) Before cleaning and (middle), after. Air can now get between to help dry the otherwise inaccessible corners and all logs are beveled to allow moisture to roll off. (Right) Same corner, another direction, after being chinked with concrete.

Chapter 16 — Chinking

Now we *are* closing in on the finish. Logs are up. Roof is on. Windows and doors in place. There will of course be things to do for a long time to come, but really now the final step is to chink ... fill all the gaps between the logs. In days of old, lotsa different things were used to accomplish this, probably the most common of which was clay mixed with grass or straw. We could have done this. We also coulda used pegs instead of spikes and split our own shingles ... but the main purpose of this book is to make things as simple as possible so that more people will see that they can do it. A few sacks of cement and a ton or so of masonry sand filled the bill. After every hard rain we don't have to worry about what washed away. But ... since the logs were put in green, after a year or so as they dry out, we may need to go behind and fill any of the tiny cracks that might appear with a caulking ... best a good silicone one ... especially at the top of the chinking between the logs. Gotta keep the moisture out, ya know.

Mixture of 1 shovel cement, 2 1/2 of sand. Mix well. Add water until just a good sticky, clay like consistency.
Mix just enough to use before it dries out too much.
Geri is wearing gloves while working with chinking. Cement is very caustic and you can burn your skin if it remains in contact with it for any period of time. Observe cautions on the cement sack.

127

(Left, top to bottom) Large gap at sloppy notch is easily taken care of with a few balls of concrete pushed, shoved & poked, inside and out, until full. (Below) Looks like more air than logs ahead of Geri.

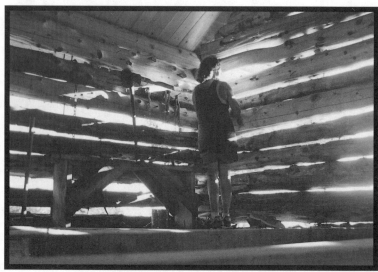

128

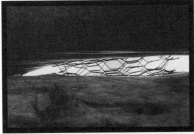

Concrete alone wasn't used to fill the spaces. Blocks of wood (top left) filled large gaps and chicken wire was used to help hold the concrete in position (L, middle and bottom). Roofing nails (short, with large heads) were also used in small spaces where concrete wouldn't fit between the logs to help keep chinking from falling out.

Look at all the windows and doors I got installed (plus five on the other two sides) while Geri was doing all of the chinking. This is one area where a helper saves a bunch of time ... like about six weeks that she did nothing but chink.

129

So there you got it.
Eight windows. Three doors.
Bought'en roofing
& other materials.
Do it yourself.
All for $3,000!

fini!

Since the main purpose of this building is to house horse gear, we built convenient to the corral.

Some of our neighbors.
Note antlers hiding
amongst dead cedar (below).

133

Old Timey Kansas Cabin

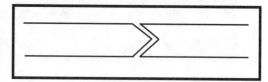

I'm so impressed with the craftsmanship of that 1870's log cabin from Blue Rapids, KS, that I had to show you once again just what can be done without the benefit of chain saws and number one quality logs.
Note their method of splicing (R).

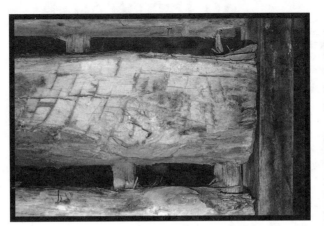

Tho it doesn't impress me enough to want to use it, the dove tail notch (left) amazes me.
No spikes readily available back then so wooden pegs made do to hold the thing together (top).
Straight limbs or saplings were used to nail to at windows and doors (right).

135

10 INDIVIDUAL BOOKLETS

#1 BRAIN TAN BUCKSKIN - still the simplest to understand, workable how-to on this subject available. Also included, how to obtain and work with sinew.

#2 PRIMITIVE FIRE &CORDAGE - learn to make string and rope from naturally found fibers, both plant and animal; bow and hand drill fire making.

#3 MAKIN' MEAT -1 SINEW BACKED BOW & ARROW - primitive bow and arrow making from raw materials. The bow illustrated being made is of the type used by the warriors of the plains.

#4 MAKIN' MEAT -2 - TRAPS & SUBSISTENCE GATHERING. Simple food gathering techniques. Also a description of the atlatl.

#5 PRIMITIVE COOKING METHODS - cooking what you catch. Boiling, broiling, baking, frying and more. All naturally.

#6 DEER, FROM FIELD TO FREEZER - The care of deer sized game. Field dress, skin, quarter, cut up - here using stone tools.

#7 CONTAINERS -1 - BASKETS, BAGS & WHAT-NOTS. It's hard to gather when you have nothing to carry your "stuff" in. Simple to learn basket weaves using natural materials. And more!

#8 CONTAINERS -2 - PRIMITIVE POTTERY - Dig your clay, clean it, build a pot and fire it. Then cook in it over an open fire.

#9 PRIMITIVE TOOLS - MAKING & USING THEM. Stone, bone, wood, antler. A well done primer on the basics of flintknapping.

#10 PRIMITIVE SEMI-PERMANENT SHELTERS - Shelters that have intregal fires and shed wind and water - from basic survival to complex houses. The very best explanation of primitive shelters available.

$4.50 each

plus $3.00 s/h (one time charge)

Primitive Wilderness Living & Survival skills

Chapter 1 — Brain Tan Buckskin
Chapter 2 — Primitive Fire & Cordage
Chapter 3 — Bow & Arrow
Chapter 4 — Traps, food gathering, etc.
Chapter 5 — Primitive Cooking Methods
Chapter 6 — Processing deer size game
Chapter 7 — Containers 1, Baskets, etc.
Chapter 8 — Containers 2, Primitive Pottery
Chapter 9 — Primitive Tools
Chapter 10 .. Primitive Semi Permanent Shelters

... here is the place to learn.
(Field & Stream)

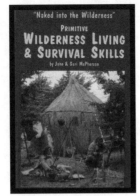

• 408 pages • 700 photos
5 1/2x8 1/2 • paperback
ISBN0897459970

This is without doubt the best training guide for real primitive living skills. *(Museum of the Fur Trade Quarterly, Vol. 31, no. 3, Fall 1995)*

— the best. — only books I have reviewed that actually work. Too many survival books are written by just copying someone else's work and in this way many mistakes, sometimes dangerous ones, are perpetuated. If you are going to purchase a survival book, get this one. I recommend it. *(Keith Burgess, outdoor writer and book reviewer, Australia)*

An Outdoor Life Book Club selection

293 pages • Loaded w/photos
5 1/2x8 1/2 • paperback
ISBN 0897459849

The authors live their subject, and their text is full of practical, tested advice for living off the land. *(Sports Afield, Winter 1997-98)*

Primitive Wilderness Skills, Applied & Advanced

Some firsts,
some only's.
Lotsa common sense!

Chapter 1 — Hantavirus
Chapter 2 — Nutrition for the primitive
Chapter 3 — Brain Tanning Robes and Furs
Chapter 4 — 20 foot Dugout Canoe, w/stone tools
Chapter 5 — Flintknapping Tips, Lighting, Bone Needle,Quick axe hafting, The Quickie Bow, Water Containers, Primitive Navigation, Two Piece Moccasin, Primitive vs. prehistoric.
Chapter 6 — Primitive, Primitive.
Chapter 7 — Naked into the Wilderness, Day 1
Chapter 8 — Naked into the Wilderness, Day 2
Chapter 9 — Naked into the Wilderness, Day 3
Chapter 10 — Storms, a short story

A new book from Prairie Wolf which will become soon a classic reference.
(International Research Survival Newsletter {France}, Dec. 1996)

VIDEOS

As with our book, we began doing videos on these skills because we found that there was not much available for you to choose from that actually worked to **teach you "how-to".** We are especially proud of the two bow videos and feel confident that these are _the_ videos to have for both the beginning and advanced bowyer.
Tapes # 1,2,3,6 & 10 are taken from chapters in our book.

#1 Brain Tan Buckskin
Step by step from fresh skin to finished buckskin in as little as 8 hours. Quickest/easiest way to accomplish this. Our most popular tape. 80 minutes.
$29.95

#2 Primitive Fire & Cordage
Three methods of friction fire and cordage from natural materials. Make your own fire by "rubbing sticks" in no time. 100 minutes.
$29.95

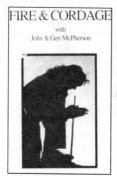

#3 Primitive Bow & Arrow
From tree to finished bow - & arrow. All steps covered - most importantly the physics explain **why & how** a stick bends. 115 minutes.
$29.95

#6 Deer - from Field to Freezer
Using only common kitchen knives, the McPhersons take a deer sized animal (a goat) from moment of kill to ready to package. 65 minutes.
$29.95

#10 Primitive Shelters
Several building techniques used to construct four different **livable semi-permanent** shelters using common litter and grasses. 90 minutes.
$29.95

#GK Asiatic Composite Bow
"How-to" construct the Asiatic Composite Bow. This is the **horn and sinew** bow that shot an arrow over half a mile - two hundred years ago. 119 minutes.
$39.95

ALSO - Save $5.00 per **large book** *(below)* - (that's 20%) - when ordering two or more at the same time -
PLUS - *on top of this save an additional 20% on all orders over $100.00*

Yes!

Please **rush** me the
items noted below!

Name
Address

City	State or Prov.	Zip

Item	Quantity	Price	Amount
Book NW-1 - "Primitive Wilderness Living & Survival Skills"		x $24.95 =	
Book NW-2 - "Primitive Wilderness Skills, Applied & Advanced"		x $24.95 =	
BOOK .... How-to Build this $3,000 Log Cabin		x $24.95 =	
Videos (please mark appropriate boxes) ☐ **#GK Asiatic Composite Bow** *(@ $39.95)*		x $39.95 =	

The below five videos come with the book (chapter) of same title.

☐ **#1 Brain Tan Buckskin** *(@ $29.95)*   ☐ **#2 Primitive Fire & Cordage** *(@ $29.95)*

☐ **#3 Primitive Bow & Arrow** *(@ $29.95)*   ☐ **#6 Field to Freezer** *(@ $29.95)*

☐ **#10 Shelters** *(@ $29.95)*

x $29.95 =	
Booklets (from above)	
Subtotal	
Minus -	
Total $	

Deduct $5.00 per large book (that's
20%) when ordering two or more at
the same time - PLUS ...
on top of this save an additional
20% on all orders over $100.00

Postage and All
applicable sales taxes included

Order from:

**Prairie Wolf
POB 96
Randolph, KS 66554**   *or*   **For fastest service call 1 (800) 258-1232**

PRIMITIVE WILDERNESS LIVING & SURVIVAL SKILLS

by John & Geri McPherson

Order Form for Booklets

Chapters as books!

YES!!!

Send me the books I have selected below at $4.50 @
(+ $3.00 s/h total)
or the
SPECIAL PRICE of *five fer four.*
(five books for the price of four).

#1 **BRAIN TAN BUCKSKIN**
#2 **PRIMITIVE FIRE & CORDAGE**
#3 **MAKIN' MEAT -1**
   SINEW BACKED BOW & ARROW
#4 **MAKIN' MEAT -2**
   TRAPS & SUBSISTENCE GATHERING
#5 **PRIMITIVE COOKING METHODS**
#6 **DEER, FROM FIELD TO FREEZER**
#7 **CONTAINERS -1**
   BASKETS, BAGS & WHATNOTS
#8 **CONTAINERS -2**
   PRIMITIVE POTTERY
#9 **PRIMITIVE TOOLS**
   MAKING & USING THEM
#10 **PRIMITIVE SEMI-PERMANENT SHELTERS**

Mark the number and quantity of book(s) desired.

#1   #6
#2   #7
#3   #8
#4   #9
#5   #10

Quantity	Price	Amount
	x $4.50 @ =	$
	x $18 (5 fer 4)	$
	s/h	$ 3.00
Total this sheet		$

Transfer this amount to the order form on the other side.

NOTES

NOTES

NOTES

NOTES